Responding to
Young Adult Literature

Responding to Young Adult Literature

Virginia R. Monseau

Boynton/Cook Publishers
HEINEMANN
Portsmouth, NH

Boynton/Cook Publishers
A subsidiary of Reed Elsevier Inc.
361 Hanover Street
Portsmouth, NH 03801-3912

Offices and agents throughout the world

Library of Congress Cataloging-in-Publication Data
Monseau, Virginia R., 1941–
    Responding to young adult literature / Virginia R. Monseau.
        p.   cm.
    Includes bibliographical references.
    ISBN 0-86709-401-X (alk. paper)
    1. Young adult literature—Study and teaching (Secondary)
  I. Title.
PN1009.A1M66   1996
    809'.89283—dc20
    [809'.89283]   96-20
                                   CIP

Editor: Peter R. Stillman
Production: Vicki Kasabian
Cover design: Jenny Jensen Greenleaf
Manufacturing: Elizabeth Valway

Printed in the United States of America on acid-free paper

Docutech OPI 2007

*For all those readers
of young adult literature*

Contents

Six
What's Age Got to Do with It? Adults Respond to Young Adult Literature

Seven
Responding to Response

Afterword

Foreword

As a writer of young adult literature, I have often been forced to consider my work a bastard child of *real* literature. As a therapist working with adolescents, I have often been forced to consider myself a bastard child of *real* therapists. I believe the two situations are connected: this culture does not give proper respect to stories about teenagers because it does not respect teenagers themselves.

Adolescence is a period in our own lives that many of us would just as soon forget, and unfortunately we often do. We look back on it, whack our foreheads with the heels of our hands, and dismiss our actions of that time as foolish and naive. Then we go on. Adolescence is so painful and embarrassing for many of us that we don't want our children or our students to experience it, would rather they learn instead from *our* experiences. We forget that adolescence is the time in which we first asked ourselves important questions, the answers for which we continue to search even today. And that forgetting is a mistake; turn your back on the source of your question and lose much of what you have to gain finding an answer.

It is self-serving to say (which is why I'll say it) that classifying literature is foolish. Putting editors into the business of marketing takes away from readers stories to which they would naturally gravitate. I am astounded at the number of letters I receive from adults who praise a certain story for the way it connects to their own lives, yet say they would never have come across the story had it not been brought to their attention by one of their children or a student. I recently read a manuscript for a so-called young adult novel, *The Watsons Go to Birmingham, 1963*, by an exquisite new writer named Christopher Curtis. (Since Mr. Curtis and I share the same first name as well as the same initials, I'm hoping readers will skim over his name and think I wrote the book.) When I flipped my computer on to write a blurb for the back of the jacket, I found myself angry that I was addressing such a limited audience. Because this book would be shelved with other young adult literature, adults wouldn't find it. Not only that, but it would be unknown to kids on the fast track in most high schools because of its YA identification. I wrote the publishers and implored them not to put juvenile cover art on this book. "Please do not do anything to limit the audience," I wrote. First Curtis bends you over with laughter, then he breaks your heart, then he gives you magic. What more could you ask of *any* novel?

Virginia Monseau addresses this issue of classification and other issues of concern to teachers and students in *Responding to Young Adult Literature*. The key idea in the title is *response*. That's what Monseau goes after and that's what she gives you. She knows that response— of the reader and of the teacher—is a key to understanding and teaching good literature. To know the information that Monseau imparts in this book is to know how to bring literature of any kind alive. And there is no line between good young adult literature and good adult literature except for the age of the protagonist.

I still remember my two correct answers on my ninth-grade exam for *The Scarlet Letter*. I nailed the color, and the actual letter. The first answer was legitimate, as I had read far enough into the title to ferret it out. The second was luck; I began my guesses at the front of the alphabet. Other than the fact that the protagonist's first name was the same as that of my great aunt on my father's side, the color and letter are, to this day, the extent of my knowledge of Hawthorne's classic. The story wasn't about anything I knew. My teacher didn't give me anything contemporary with which to compare the complex issues addressed in the book, something that would have helped me relate those issues to my life. With that assignment, reading became something that was no longer fun for me. When it stopped being fun, I stopped doing it.

Like it or not, a healthy adolescence is a time of separation, a time of rebellion. To concerned adults it may seem a time of sullenness, of turning away; but in that sullenness, in that search for privacy, adolescence is also a time to begin asking the questions that good literature through the ages has asked and answered. Who am I? What is the nature of good and evil? Of free will? What adults need to remember is that we, too, began asking those questions in that time. And we probably haven't yet answered them all. It might help us even now to listen to a Holden Caulfield or a Sarabeth Silver or a Bert Bowden or a Billy Baggs as they walk that treacherous ground toward adulthood.

Several years ago I wrote a so-called adult novel, called *The Deep End;* I am currently writing another. For me, there is no difference in the storytelling between the adult and young adult genres. Virginia Monseau, in this book, highlights that truth. She asks us to elevate all good literature to the same place and to judge it by the same standards, to judge it by readers' response.

In my work as a therapist with teenagers, I have encountered a number of bright kids from "good" homes who are in advanced placement classes and headed for the best colleges. They share many of the same fears and worries about the future—as well as the present—that less-advantaged teens face. They often look at high school education as some detached entity that they have to endure in order to get into college and come out prepared for the world of work. The pressure is on. I believe that the teaching of literature offers us as educators a chance to make a connection with these kids. By sharing our responses to stories about lives like theirs, and by relating our own lives to those stories, we can bring their education home, make it an intimate thing. By not making a connection between the issues dealt with in the classics and the issues dealt with in good young adult literature, we too often pass up that opportunity.

I hope that one day kids will balk at reading—or outright refuse to read—my work because I am long dead and my stories are out of step with "kids today," and that educators will use contemporary stories to bring my meanings home. That will mean that the world is moving along as it should. It will mean that my work is being passed over, or at least pushed aside, for the work of vibrant new authors, a few of whom might have been inspired by parents or teachers who were themselves long ago inspired by my work.

Apart from being informative, *Responding to Young Adult Literature* is a how-to book that I, as a writer of young adult fiction, embrace because it points out how to treat my work, and the work of scores of others like me, in a way that maximizes the worth of young adult literature.

Chris Crutcher

Preface

Contemporary young adult literature has been around in one form or another for more than fifty years, yet school curricula are slow to reflect its emergence into the reading lives of young people and its acceptance as an object of critical study. Why is this so? Part of the answer, I believe, lies in the stigma that has been attached to this literature over the years—the assumption that, because it appeals to adolescents, young adult literature can't possibly be worthy of a place in the English curriculum. Though disturbing, such an attitude is not surprising, when we think of the skepticism with which African American literature, women's literature, working class literature, and the literature of other groups labeled as minorities have been received by the literary establishment. There will always be those Brahmins who look askance at any literature enjoyed (and understood) by the masses, but when educators adopt this mindset, we have cause for concern.

There is another reason schools have failed to recognize the value of young adult literature to the curriculum: ignorance of the power this literature has to evoke in students the kind of literary experience that will keep them reading and lead them to a deeper understanding of literature in general, and the relationship between literature and life in particular. Classroom study of literature is mostly teacher-talk interspersed with student answers to teacher-conceived questions about complex literary works. Little, if any, attention is paid to the effect of the reading on the student or to the consequences of that literary transaction. Though most teachers want their students to learn to love literature, few are willing to address this question: How can students have a literary experience with a work they do not understand? That is why I have written this book—to help English teachers see what can happen when students are given the opportunity to read young adult literature, and simultaneously to demonstrate how a response approach to the literature might work in the classroom. In an effort to establish young adult literature as a genre worthy of study, I have also included the responses of teachers and other adults to various young adult novels, some of which were read and discussed by the students I've worked with.

Ten years ago, I spent several months reading and talking about young adult literature with groups of high school students and their English teachers. The transcripts of our discussions became part of my doctoral dissertation and, in fact, are still valuable to me today as I read young adult literature with my college students and try to understand its significance to the young people whose lives are reflected in its pages. The responses of their teachers, too, are important to me, for they often reveal underlying attitudes and expectations that influence whether and how the literature is read and studied in the classroom. Equally important, teacher response, and the responses of other adults, may provide clues to the degree of universality inherent in this literature that is marketed specifically for young adults.

Though I've often talked to teachers who are students in my graduate classes about their reading of young adult literature, other professional commitments have slowed my quest to learn more about how young adults themselves read and how their reading influences their learning. Remembering those stimulating discussions of a decade ago, I've felt some pangs of regret at my failure to maintain a more sustained dialogue with young adult readers over the years.

Of particular interest to me, for example, is the value of YA literature to students of varying academic abilities. If young adult literature is included in the curriculum at all, it is usually in the basic English class, which is populated largely by readers dubiously labeled as "reluctant." The philosophy seems to be, "Since these students can't read 'real' literature, let's give them something they *can* read, something simple that doesn't demand much of the reader." Aside from the fact that such a rationale reveals an ignorance about young adult literature itself, this kind of elitist justification does a dangerous disservice to students. In addition to perpetuating the labeling that's already all too familiar to them, such an attitude demeans them as readers, assuming that because they *will not* read, they *cannot* read.

Also intriguing to me is the role of young adult literature in students' goals for study. This brings us to the other end of the spectrum, the "smart" students in honors and advanced placement classes. They, of course, are the "good" readers—or at least we assume they are. Striving to earn the A's they feel are essential, these students read and write about the literary masterpieces, trying to guess what their teachers want, hoping to prepare themselves for the college entrance tests that loom on the horizon. For the most part, these students don't encounter young adult literature in school, the assumption being that it's too easy for them and doesn't present much of a challenge. (And, of course, it doesn't appear on standardized tests—an issue I explored with these students in my research.) What would happen, I wondered, if advanced students *did* read young adult literature in their classes? Would they consider it a waste of time, or would they find it useful to their goals for literary study? I also wondered what might occur if the so-called reluctant readers and the advanced students got together to respond to a young adult novel. Who would say what to whom, and with what result? These are the questions I address in Chapters 1, 2, and 3. (Note: Though tracking is a controversial issue among educators, my research depended upon such academic grouping; thus, I worked with students and teachers whose classes were grouped according to ability.)

Though I sought the answers to my questions in the classroom, there are other questions of interest to me, the answers to which can be found only outside of class. How do adolescents respond to young adult literature that they read for pure enjoyment, with no concern about tests or grades? And how might this out-of-class response inform literary study in the classroom? For the past several years I have been involved in a school-university articulation project called the Youngstown State University English Festival. Each year students from area schools come to the university campus over a three-day period to take part in a variety of reading, writing, and discussion activities based on a reading list of seven young adult books. The writing done in response to these books provides insight into the students' strategies for making meaning. I examine some of their efforts and those of their teachers in Chapters 4, 5, and 6. Knowledge of what these readers find significant in a literary work may prove valuable to the study of literature in the classroom.

Many of the books and articles written about student response to literature focus on techniques or methods that teachers can use to evoke that response. With this book I want to concentrate on the readers themselves—students, teachers, and other adults—describing their responses in different situations and inviting you, the reader, to explore the significance of these responses with me in Chapter 7. Marilyn Hanf Buckley is right when she says

> It has not been the educators' style to learn from their subject, that is, the student, the way other scientists do. Astronomers study stars, botanists plants, but teachers do not study children. Our arrogance has kept us ignorant. Without such study, what we say about learning is suspect. (57)

For our purposes, we might add the word *adults* to Buckley's list, remembering that not all students are children.

So, with the help of a sabbatical from Youngstown State University and a grant from the ALAN Foundation (The Assembly on Literature for Adolescents of the National Council of Teachers of English), I offer this book. My wish is to bring you into the reading worlds of adolescents and adults so that you may observe their struggle to make meaning of young adult literature. Additionally, I hope that my examination of journals, essays, and poems written by young adults and their teachers in response to YA literature will provide further insight into the transaction between reader and text.

I thank the following people who assisted in my research: Maxine Houck, Melanie Loew, Jane Price, Albert Tucciarone, and Rick Williams. I'm grateful to the teachers who let me come into their classrooms to listen and learn. I'm also indebted to their students, who patiently tolerated my intrusions and willingly read, discussed, and wrote for me. I appreciate the help of Thomas Gay and Gary Salvner, past and present chairs of the YSU English Festival, for making archival material available to me. And, as always, I thank my family—Paul, Michele, and Jennifer—for their encouragement and support, especially when the Muse refused to visit.

Work Cited

Buckley, Marilyn Hanf. 1982. "Falling into the White Between the Black Lines." In *Reader Response in the Classroom: Evoking and Interpreting Meaning in Literature*, ed. Nicholas J. Karolides, 45-58. New York: Longman.

One

Having Their Say: Responding to Young Adult Literature in the Basic English Class

My response to [my parents'] appreciation of the written word was to read a grand total of one book from cover to cover during my entire four years of high school, opting rather to invent titles for book reports, as well as stories to go with them, and choosing the names of the authors from the pages of the Boise telephone directory.

Chris Crutcher

This admission by Chris Crutcher, celebrated author of books for young adults, might bring a smile to the faces of adults who remember similar school experiences, just as it might shock some teachers who assume that all authors are longtime book lovers. But the people who might be influenced the most by Crutcher's confession are students labeled reluctant readers, who may also mistakenly believe that all authors are former honor students who never met a book they didn't like. Crutcher's words give hope to these young readers and to the teachers who may have given up on them.

I was one of those teachers. Until the day I sat in on Jean Foster's class. Jean taught all of the bottom-track ninth graders at her school, and she had agreed to take part in my research on response to young adult literature. Interested in using YA literature with her students but

unable to afford extra paperbacks, she jumped at my offer to provide
her with a class set of any book she chose. A discussion Jean and I had
with Marcia and Elizabeth, who taught the honors and advanced
placement students and who were also to take part in the study,
resulted in a decision to use Robert Cormier's *After the First Death*. A
complex, riveting novel of intrigue, the story involves three young
protagonists—each touched in some way by the others and each
deceived by trusted adults. Kate, a bright, beautiful young woman, is
substituting for her uncle, driving a busload of preschool children to
day camp. Miro, a young terrorist who is part of a plan to hijack the
bus and hold the children hostage in return for military favors, is
charged with killing the bus driver—his first death. Ben, the teenage
son of General Marcus Marchand, is used by his father as a decoy to
fool the terrorists into thinking the army is meeting their demands. As
the plot unfolds, readers come to know each of these young characters through alternating chapters in which Cormier weaves their lives
together in preparation for the devastating chain of events that follow.

All three teachers believed the novel would be interesting and
challenging enough to be enjoyed by all the students, regardless of
their perceived ability. Jean, however, expressed concern about her
students' ability and willingness to read the book in its entirety, citing
their poor reading skills and apathy. To circumvent anticipated problems, she decided to read portions of the novel aloud to her students
each day, and to quiz them with recall questions as she went along.
Our plan was that I would sit in on one of Jean's classes during a discussion of the book after she had finished reading it to them. I made
it clear that I didn't want to direct the discussion, but instead wanted
to be just another participant. Jean insisted on using her best-behaved
class, but she cautioned me not to expect too much. As it turned out,
I wasn't disappointed in her students' abilities or interest.

I had recently read Vine and Faust's *Situating Readers: Students
Making Meaning of Literature*, and what I learned from the class discussion reinforced Vine and Faust's theory that "successful readers are
situated readers who begin by asking questions such as: What's going
on here? Who's doing what, how, to what effect, and why?" (107).
They explain further:

> Being situated . . . encompasses much more than merely possessing
> appropriate linguistic and other cultural knowledge. To be situated is
> to be aware of ourselves engaged in experiencing a particular situa-
> tion, at a particular time, with particular other people, and with par-
> ticular purposes in mind, realizing that our sense of this particular
> situation is potentially influenced by all the previous voices and
> experiences that affect how we interpret the world and how we see
> ourselves. Thus, for instance, each member of the same social group

experiencing a familiar cultural situation may share a common sense of its general nature, yet have a different sense of its particular meaning. These social and personal aspects of meaning making ought to be acknowledged . . . as integral—not peripheral—to a clear understanding of what people do when they read. (139)

Several of the basic ninth graders with whom I discussed *After the First Death* showed evidence of being "situated" in this sense. One young man, Jason, was obviously quite engaged with the book, eager to answer his teacher's questions and to ask a few of his own.

The day I visited Jean's classroom, only eight of the fifteen students were present. The small group proved ideal for discussion. As we moved our chairs into a circle, Jean began by reviewing plot events that the class had discussed the previous day, asking a series of recall questions that she hoped would encourage the students' participation.

Jean: What time was the attack supposed to happen? Where did we end yesterday? Jason?

Jason: 9:30.

Jean: At 9:30. That's what Ben tells the terrorists. How does Ben tell them? What kind of situation?

Jason: The fingers.

Jean: He's being tortured.

Jason: Right. (*Another student, Emily, asks an inaudible question.*)

Jean: Let's see if we can help Emily out a little bit here. Can we?

Jason: May I ask a question, please?

Jean: Sure.

Jason: He has crippled fingers, right, this Artkin? A crippled hand? Does he do some kind of death pinch on Ben?

Jean: I think that the reason Cormier stays so vague on that is that he's just leaving us a little leeway to . . . imagine . . .

Jason: Imagine . . . yeah. (*Student and teacher talk simultaneously.*)

Jean: Okay. Let's get the rest of the class caught up with us. After Kate first tries to steal the bus, what's the first thing Artkin does?

Jason: Blames Miro.

Jean: Blames Miro. What saves Miro, though?

Jason: It was Artkin's fault, also, for leaving Miro in charge of the bus. Something along that line.

Jason's question about "the fingers" is never really answered here, and he doesn't persist in exploring it further. His spark of interest has apparently been doused by factual questions that tap only lower-level thinking skills—the kind of questions frequently asked of students in basic classes. It is obvious that Jason's fourteen-year-old mind is curious about the method used for torturing Ben, and that he wants to better understand just what Ben went through. Jason was certainly a "situated reader" according to Vine and Faust's definition, yet lack of teacher awareness of what it means to be a "situated reader" could make it easy to dismiss his question as idle curiosity. Further evidence of Jason's and other students' meaning making occurred as the discussion progressed.

Jean: Do you remember we talked about the "messenger gambit"? What was the "messenger gambit"?

Emily: Oh, that was Ben.

Jean: Ben, okay. What was the plan for the messenger gambit? To do what?

Jason: To gamble a little bit with the children . . . not with the children, but . . . he said, the guy told him, the general said, "I'll give you my own son to assure that we don't mean any harm."

Jean: Exactly. So Ben is the messenger.

Jason: And his father's gambling with his life.

Jean: Do we know the whole plan, though? As of right now, do we know the whole . . .

Jason (*interrupts*): Yeah, now we do—or *I* do, anyway.

Jean (*laughs*): Yes, *you* do. And we all will soon.

Sitting next to Jason during this discussion, I could feel his eagerness to let everyone know his interpretation of the plot. He wanted to keep talking, and he became visibly annoyed that other students couldn't participate in the discussion because they hadn't finished the book.

Jean: Melinda, how far are you?

Melinda (*almost inaudible*): I didn't finish it . . .

Jean: We had a few people who were on a band trip. They were supposed to read it, but . . .

Jason (*to Melinda*): Why didn't you read it on the bus?

Melinda: There was too much noise.

Jason: That's just an excuse.

Jason's annoyance may have stemmed in part from the whispered questions that Melinda kept asking Jean during the discussion. Melinda seemed to be interested in the character Kate, but she wasn't comfortable asking her questions of the group.

Although Jason was obviously engaged by the book, when the students began reading sections of the novel aloud, he proved to be one of the least fluent readers. He frequently stumbled over words, reading haltingly and with little expression, and Jean sometimes had to fill in words for him. This brought to mind Frank Smith's admonition in his book *Reading Without Nonsense,* where he points out that reading is a meaning-making activity rather than a "sound" activity. I wondered whether Jason had been in the "bottom group" since primary school partly because his lack of skill at reading *aloud* had been interpreted as a lack of *comprehension.* Despite his lack of fluency, Jason knew just about every plot detail in the book, and he knew just where to look when discussion turned to the death of the character Ben.

Jean: How did Ben die?

Derek: He jumped off Brimmler's Bridge. He committed suicide.

Jason didn't buy this. He blamed Ben's death on Ben's father. Quickly searching for evidence, he read from the book Ben's words to his father, "You killed me twice."

Jason: That's what it is. He sent him on the bridge on a suicide mission, and then he drove him to suicide.

Derek: It's his dad from the beginning.

Jean: What do you mean?

Derek: It's his dad telling the story. He committed suicide, too.

Jean: But the father's not dead at the end of the book.

Derek: But something died in his father. A part of him died.

I was impressed, to say the least. Here was a group of supposedly reluctant readers, reading a complicated novel, the structure of which still puzzles teachers and scholars, and showing remarkable insight into the novel's most complex elements. The manner of Ben's death and the confusion of the Ben/General voice are two of the most difficult aspects of the novel, yet the students had cut to the heart of the book's significance. What was going on?

I believe that, first of all, the students were delighted to be reading a book that didn't talk down to them—a book that challenged them to make sense of it and at the same time captured their interest in the plot and characters. The characters Kate, Ben, and Miro are innocent adolescents caught in a web of manipulation, violence, and intrigue woven by adults whom they trust. As young adults still seeking their identity, Kate, Ben, and Miro represent every adolescent who labors to understand life and its meaning. Their conflicts are experienced by all young adults, irrespective of intellectual ability or social status. In these characters Cormier has created young people whom readers love, despise, cheer, and mourn. In a questionnaire, I asked Jean's students, "If you could write a letter to a character in

After the First Death, who would it be and why?" Of the thirteen who
responded, six said they would write to Miro, four to Kate, two to
Ben, and one to Artkin. The reasons they gave included

- I would ask Miro why he did what he did. I would tell him
  that if he's trying to be a man, doing this isn't being a man.
- I want to ask Miro why he shot the girl at the end.
- I would write Miro to see why he's such an angry man.
- I would write to Kate because she had so much courage and
  never chickened out. She had two sides to her and always
  stayed under control.
- I'll write to Kate because I think I am like her. I'm trying to
  find the bravery in myself.

In addition to the engagement that is evident in their responses,
these students showed pride in reading a book that was not "watered
down" or "immature." Jean told me early in the project that one of
her students had approached her before class one day and in a surprised whisper asked, "Did you know that the kids in the advanced
class are reading this book, too?" (The student wasn't aware that we
planned to combine the advanced and basic classes to work collaboratively on a project that focused on *After the First Death.*)

Collaboration Between Basic and Advanced Ninth Graders

The idea for collaboration stemmed from my curiosity about what
would happen if students in the bottom and top tracks were asked to
work together on a reading/writing task. Fortunately, Jean and Marcia,
who taught the advanced ninth graders, shared my curiosity and
agreed to combine both groups to collaborate on a literature simulation
called "Hit Vids!" (See Chapter 4 for more information on such simulations.) The instructions called for the creation of a music video starring a character from *After the First Death.* We decided it would be best
if the students worked on neutral ground rather than in one classroom
or the other, so we met in the school library. We assigned them to
groups of four, mixing students from both classes. Each group was told
to select a character from the novel, decide what kind of music that
person would write and perform (rock, country, heavy metal, etc.),
write the lyrics to a song the character would create based on the events
of the novel, give the song and video a title, describe what would occur
in the music video, and draw a scene from the video that would appear
on the cover of the videotape—all in a forty-five minute period.

Any concern we had about the students working together vanished as they immediately got to work. As I circulated among the groups, I observed the following:

- The artist in the group was frequently a student in the basic class.
- The writer was most often a student in the advanced class.
- When there was a disagreement about which type of music a character would write, the decision was made irrespective of track. (Example: Our friend Jason from the basic class felt that Miro would sing heavy metal; the others—all from the advanced group—thought that Miro would write a spiritual. After much discussion they settled on heavy metal.)
- The students seemed to respect each other's ability to do certain tasks. (Example: As I eavesdropped, I saw Jason dictating the lyrics of the song "Killer on the Road" as one of Marcia's students wrote them down. The others in the group offered their suggestions, which Jason either accepted or rejected, depending on how well they fit his idea of what the song should be.)
- All but one group chose the young terrorist Miro as its singer-songwriter, creating songs such as "I Shot the Bus Driver," "Venom Juice," and "Hijacking Blues." Only one group chose Ben, whose song was entitled "Failing Once Again."

My first and second observations were not surprising. Students in basic classes often feel more comfortable with a pictorial representation of what they have learned than with a written representation. That several of the basic students volunteered to be the artist when their groups divided the tasks is telling. Whether they lacked confidence in their writing, didn't like to write, or just enjoyed drawing, these students preferred using pictures rather than words to show what they knew about the book. (This wasn't entirely true of Jason, however, as we will see later.) Conversely, students who are comfortable with writing usually have no problem taking on new writing tasks, and this was evident as, in most groups, it was an advanced student who wrote down ideas for the video as the group brainstormed. Though everyone in the group contributed to the discussion, the writer maintained control of what went on the paper, in most cases writing the lyrics of the song in poetic stanza form.

Each group's conversation focused first on character, as the students tried to decide who would become the subject of their music video. They then discussed the plot of the novel to establish which events were most significant for their particular character. The titles the students chose for their songs reveal which events they decided to focus on.

That most of the groups chose Miro as their singer-songwriter is intriguing for two reasons. First, he is one of the bad guys in the novel. His sole desire at first is to kill Kate, the young female protagonist. Second, his unwavering loyalty to a cause that he does not completely understand is often puzzling to young adult readers who are unaware of the influence that a repressive culture can have upon behavior. Did their choice reflect a certain identification with Miro, or did it merely stem from an adolescent attraction to tough, violent behavior? It's impossible to be certain, but I suspect it's more the former than the latter. Cormier has created in Miro a character who cannot be dismissed as merely bad. Young adult readers are quick to pick up on qualities in Miro with which they empathize: his physical attraction to Kate; his fascination with Elvis Presley; his manipulation by Artkin, the adult terrorist whom he admires. Though they may not be consciously aware of it, readers seem to sense the innocence in Miro that Cormier portrays so well. He is a fascinating character, and choosing him as their singer-songwriter gave students an opportunity to explore why and how he fascinated them so much.

This may also explain why the remaining group chose Ben as its subject, for he is the most puzzling character in the novel. In their written responses to the book, many students said they wanted to know how Ben died—and why his father used him as a decoy. While they felt sorry for Ben, they wondered why he didn't question his father more and why he let himself be manipulated. The title of Ben's song, "Failing Once Again," indicates the group's overall impression of this young man who, sadly, fulfills his father's expectation of weakness.

The dynamics of each group discussion were interesting to watch. Although I was pleased to see that everyone participated, I noticed that some of Jean's students seemed content to say less and let the others make decisions about their video. As I noted earlier, however, Jason was not one of these. From the very beginning, it was apparent that he had his own ideas about how this video would turn out. Unlike some of the others in his class, he didn't shy away from using words, though he preferred not to be the one to write them down. Trying to be unobtrusive, I listened as Jason tried different versions of certain lines from "Killer on the Road," trying to decide, for example, whether the song should be called "Killer on the Run" instead, or whether the last line of the chorus should be "He'll shoot you in the head," rather than "He'll kill you in your head." His decision to keep the title "Killer on the Road" was made to emphasize that Miro is still "out there somewhere" waiting to kill someone else. "Killer on the Run," Jason felt, suggested that Miro was running from the authorities—period. And though Jason didn't articulate it quite this way, he felt that the phrase "He'll kill you in your head" suggested a psychological element, while "He'll shoot you in the head" represented merely a one-time violent action. The others in the group seemed content with Jason's reasoning and experimented with the lyrics. The final version of the song consisted of three verses and a chorus:

CHORUS: Killer on the road has got you in his sight.
              He stalks you day and night.
              Just like a monster under your bed,
              He'll kill you in your head.

VERSE 1:   One day you're riding on a bus,
              'till some guys start to make a fuss.
              They take you hostage, passing out candy.
              You feel high, and sleep is dandy.
              You wake up crying for your mom,
              But you know that she's long gone.

CHORUS

VERSE 2:   The bus driver tries to find out if she's brave,
              But not too much or they'll lay her in a grave.
              The messenger Ben tries to make peace,
              But he made Artkin mad, now he's going to cease.

CHORUS

VERSE 3:   The army's on the scene; they're hard and they're
                mean.
              The kids are saved, but Kate's in her grave.
              Who could have figured? I pulled the trigger.
              Now I'm on the run; my only friend's my gun.

CHORUS

Another group—which ended up as a pair, since two students had to leave early—decided to make Miro a rhythm and blues singer. The students, a young woman from Jean's class and a young man from Marcia's, worked diligently to come up with lyrics that would portray Miro's confusion about his attraction to Kate and his duty as a terrorist. They called their song "Hijacking Blues."

        I'm from this little country
        That I've never even seen.
        I'm made fun of by my boss
        Just because he's very mean.
        I met this pretty woman
        She was fine, as you can see.

But in reality I should know
That it just can never be.
There are all these bratty kids
They're really getting on my nerves.
And I just can't get over
All those American curves.
I just saw my picture on the evening news.
That gave me more of those hijacking blues.

The production script of this pair's music video read as follows:

Song Title: Hijacking Blues
Performed By: Miro and the Terrors
Cast: Stroll (drummer); Antibbe (bass guitar); Artkin (lead guitar); Miro (lead singer)
Setting for Video: A smoky nightclub called "Hijackers' Hideaway" in the terrorists' home country
Action: The group is on a stage singing and playing, and they have guns hidden in their jacket pockets. In the middle of the song they pull out their guns, shoot into the air to quiet the crowd, and begin to pass out candy. The audience eats the candy and falls asleep as the song finishes and the video fades out.

The students' drawing for the video jacket, one of the most clever done by any group, depicted the outside of the nightclub "Hijackers' Hideaway," which featured a sign that read:

TONIGHT! ONE NIGHT ONLY!
BE TAKEN HOSTAGE BY PROFESSIONAL TERRORISTS

What Do We Do with Students like Jason?

That ninth graders—or anyone for that matter—could complete this collaborative activity so successfully in forty-five minutes is impressive. That these students worked together across learning tracks is even more noteworthy, since their cooperation and ultimate success debunk some of the myths about literacy and learning that circulate among educators. For example, Jason's engagement with *After the First Death*, his insights about the book, and his excitement at having the opportunity to make those insights public contradict the image of the bottom track student who either can't or won't read, shows little interest in discussion, and possesses poor language skills. Just as we encourage our students to take ownership of their writing, Jason took ownership of the song he created for Miro, though he "wrote" it orally. When his group took its turn presenting its singer-songwriter to the class, it was Jason who stepped to the front and read the song lyrics aloud. He was obviously proud. How often do we see that in a basic English class? Was it the simulation/game aspect of the exercise that excited Jason? Was it the novel itself? Was it the chance to work with the advanced students? Was it the fact that he could show off a little? Any of these reasons would be enough to warrant reexamining our assumptions about reluctant learners.

What do we do with students like Jason? Are they really being served in a basic English class where little is expected of them? Are we as teachers contributing to their literacy, or are they literate in spite of us? On a final questionnaire I gave to the students, I asked the question, "What do you read for pleasure, outside of school?" Nine of the thirteen who responded listed various books, magazines, and newspapers, while only four said "Nothing" or "I don't like to read." To my question, "What do you think would be the ideal English class?" I received answers like "Reading enjoyable books," "A class with nothing but reading," and "Read novels all the time and discuss them in class as a group." Only four students replied that they would prefer to do nothing. A few students also commented that they would like to read more "mature things," like *After the First Death*, in their English class.

I spoke with Marcia, the teacher of the advanced class, and expressed my frustration that students like Jason, once they are consigned to the bottom track, seem doomed to stay there throughout their school years. Marcia replied that, even if such students were placed in a higher track, they wouldn't be able to do the work. "They'd just fail," she said, referring to their poor study habits and low-level writing and thinking skills. Disappointed by her response at first, I continued to listen as she offered an alternative. "What we need is to develop a curriculum for these students using more books like *After the First Death*," Marcia said, "books the students will read and want to write about. No one seems to take the time to do that."

Yes, and isn't that the point? These are the students who need more from us, and in response to that need we give them less—less thought, less care, less respect, less engaging material. And lest I sound like a bleeding heart, I know all the stories about indifference, poor attendance, drug and alcohol abuse, and bad behavior. I've been there. I've had students throw up their "liquid lunch" of alcohol in my sixth-period class. I've refereed a spitting fight between two chronic suspendees. I've been on the receiving end of vulgar language from students after I've phoned parents about classroom infractions. And I've been guilty of feeling sorry for myself for being burdened with "impossible" students. Only now, after I've left all those ninth graders behind, only now, when I've been able to put some distance between me and them, only now do I realize how much more I could have done, but didn't.

When I began my research, Jason's teacher told me that he was a troublemaker in class. She wanted to forewarn me, in case he caused any problems in our discussion group. "Uh-oh," I thought, "he's going to ruin everything." (How ready I was to believe the worst.) He may have been on his best behavior when I was there, but he certainly didn't live up to his reputation. I've always believed, as many experts have testified, that disruptive behavior is tied to boredom and lack of self-esteem. In the bottom-track classes, I think it's also an attempt to promote the negative image that these students are so conscious of carrying.

What we need is someone to champion reluctant learners. No, we can't fix their family problems or cure their addictions (and not all reluctant learners have these troubles), but we *can* give them a curriculum that excites them and challenges them to learn. These students know instinctively when we're insulting their intelligence. They just don't feel it's worth the effort to articulate their frustration and anger. We make it too easy for them to wear the "I don't care" shell that they carry around in self-defense.

Young adult literature isn't the answer to all curricular problems in the basic English class, but its effectiveness has been proven time and again. As important as the literature itself are the way in which it is presented and the teacher who presents it. Using young adult literature with reluctant readers is nothing new, but creating intellectual challenges for students through the literature and rewarding their insights does not happen nearly as often as it ought to.

Works Cited

Cormier, R. 1979. *After the First Death*. New York: Dell.

Smith, F. 1985. *Reading Without Nonsense*, 2nd ed. New York: Teachers College Press.

Vine, H. A., Jr., and M. A. Faust. 1993. *Situating Readers: Students Making Meaning of Literature*. Urbana, IL: National Council of Teachers of English.

Two

More Than an Easy Read: Responding to Young Adult Literature in the Honors Class

*So much of what we call education has to do with stuffing infor-
mation into young heads and then checking on it periodically to
see whether it's stayed put or fallen out. But what about what's
already in there—observations, interpretations, imagination,
vision, emotion?*

Sandy Asher

Ninth graders can be strange creatures. One day they're cool and
aloof, trying hard to appear sophisticated and worldly; the next day
they're a bundle of emotions, crying or fighting at the slightest prov-
ocation. When they're in their "cool" mode, it's usually futile to hope
for a revealing response to what they read; they don't ever want to be
caught sounding stupid. And when they're highly emotional, they're
sometimes too preoccupied to respond at all; broken hearts and broken friendships take priority. If we're lucky, educators can catch students at an in-between stage, where life is primarily good and literature helps them explore it. Fortunately, not all ninth graders are in
the same mode at the same time, so teachers can reasonably expect
some degree of response from their students, depending on the catalyst for that response. In a class populated by advanced ninth graders,
this catalyst can be especially significant.

The Responses of Advanced Ninth Graders

Most students in honors or advanced classes are there because of high test scores and teacher recommendations. They are usually goal-oriented achievers who are willing to work hard to earn the grades that will get them into the college of their choice. The English curriculum for such students has traditionally consisted primarily of great works of literature and, ideally, a good amount of writing. But in addition to requiring the study of the Romantic poets, Dickens, and Shakespeare, some progressive teachers are now giving their advanced students the opportunity to seriously study young adult literature, realizing its potential for students' literary growth. These teachers are paying attention to recent research and scholarship that support the use of young adult literature with advanced students.

Marcia is such a teacher. Her students, as we saw in Chapter 1, read Cormier's *After the First Death*. In addition to collaborating with the students in Jean's basic-level class, they reacted in other ways to Cormier's book. For example, as an alternative to whole-class discussion, and because Cormier's complex plot structure can be confusing to even the most sophisticated reader, Marcia had her students work in small groups developing time lines for the novel. As the students talked, they helped each other better understand the novel's events. One student, for example, was confused about whose "time" they were talking about:

Marissa: Is this Cormier time or our time?

Chad: It's normal time, right?

Michael: Yeah, that's what it is.

Chad: They send their demands, drug the children.

Marissa: The girl tries to escape.

Leeann: That's after the demands.

Marissa: Who's killed?

Chad: Raymond is killed—and Kevin.

Marissa: And what about the two guys, Stroll and . . .

Chad: . . . Antibbe, and then Artkin's killed, which is Miro's first death.

Uncertain about the accuracy of this assumption, the group called on Marcia for help.

Chad (*to Marcia*): Didn't Miro consider his first death Artkin, because he never warned him?

Marcia: Miro went onto the bus believing his first death would be the . . .

Chad: . . . . girl.

Marcia: . . . . bus driver.

Chad: But it ended up being Artkin because he never warned him of . . .

Marcia (*interrupts*): Chapter 12—doesn't he say that? It was supposed to be Kate.

Chad: I think.

Marcia: And if you're dealing again with the literal, or by association . . .

Michael (*interrupts*): I never got that part . . .

Chad(*interrupts*): He ends up killing Kate anyway.

Marcia: *There's* a test question. Was it Kate, or was it Artkin?

Chad: It was Artkin, wasn't it?

It's interesting that Marcia thought in terms of test questions, while the students were trying to disentangle Cormier's plot. It is also interesting that, even after talking briefly with his teacher, Chad continued to be uncertain about his own conviction that Miro's "first death" was Artkin and not Kate. Cormier is deliberately ambiguous about this plot event, leaving it up to the reader to make a case for either interpretation. Perhaps Chad didn't have enough faith in himself as a reader to make his last comment an assertion rather than a question.

Another group in Marcia's class was particularly interested in the character Ben Marchand, who was heartlessly used by his father, General Marcus Marchand, as a decoy to dupe the terrorists who were holding Kate and the children hostage. The novel is ambiguous about whether Ben is dead or alive and whether it is, in fact, he who is telling the story.

Leslie (*confused*): Ben's dead and he's writing about his dad?

Kara: No, he runs away after his dad visits [him at school].

Leslie: John said Ben got shot.

Kara: No, he got shot, but he's talking about, like in the beginning of the book, where he has . . .

Leslie (*interrupts*): Yeah, but we're doing this in order, though.

Rebecca: No, he's already dead. He's writing as a ghost . . .

Leslie: Really?

Rebecca: Yeah, because right here it says he has a hole . . .

Leslie (*interrupts*): A hole in his heart?

Rebecca: Yeah, but it's, like, already covered up. (*Reads from book*) "I have a tunnel in my chest."

John (*back to the time line*): Okay. What about dad? Dad visits?

Rebecca: Ben dying, should we say?

Kara: Yeah.

Rebecca (*writing*): Ben jumps off bridge.

John: What about that one part, the fingers?

Kara: Yeah. What did they do? They were, like, strangling him?

Leslie (*incredulous*): Yeah!

Andy: They didn't say what it was.

John: Conscience.

Kara: His dad's conscience.

Rebecca: Dad brings up Ben in his conscience?

Kara: In the presence of his conscience.

Rebecca (*writing*): Dad . . .

John: . . . talks to Ben in his mind.

Kara (*satisfied*): There you go!

The verbal collaboration among these students as they made sense of Cormier's plot—finishing each other's sentences, answering each other's questions, experimenting with words—led them to a better understanding of the work. Constructing a time line may not at first seem like personal response to literature, but we can see that this discussion allowed the readers the freedom to interpret and question, and sometimes resulted in their returning to the text for verification. This is exactly the kind of discussion Louise Rosenblatt advocates:

> Though a free, uninhibited emotional reaction to a work of art or literature is an absolutely *necessary* condition of sound literary judgment, it is not, to use the logician's term, a *sufficient* condition. Without a real impact between the book and the mind of the reader, there can be no process of judgment at all . . . [The reader] can begin to achieve a sound approach to literature only when he reflects upon his response to it, when he attempts to understand what in the work and in himself produced that reaction, and when he thoughtfully goes on to modify, reject, or accept it. (75–76)

Satisfied by the time line exercise that her students had a firm grasp of Cormier's plot, Marcia moved on to characterization, inviting the students to work in groups using free association. They were to think metaphorically, connecting the novel's characters to things with which they were familiar—colors, shapes, animals, objects, etc. Though Marcia didn't prescribe a specific structure, she asked the students to follow the mention of each object with a metaphorical statement connecting the object to the novel.

After brainstorming, each group composed a poem about one particular character from *After the First Death*. A group that chose Miro wrote:

Miro

a VCR
mentally recording Artkin's beliefs
silly putty
imprinting and distorting freedom
salt water
transparent and turbulent
purple
bruised inside and out
an amorphous blob
without boundaries
a tragic journal
revealing a horrific past
a maggot-infested apple
vulnerable host for a parasite
a kangaroo
pouched inside Artkin
a caution flasher
pulsing suppressed emotions

Capturing the essence of Kate, another group chose appropriate images:

Kate

a yellow puddle of urine
A Betsy Wetsy doll
urinates underpants
a hyphen
stuck in the middle of the situation
a strainer
separating children from terrorists
a strawberry
sweet but sometimes sour
a kangaroo
comforting the children
a warm glass of milk
relieving children's fears
a heart
not giving up, always caring

A third group composed a poem about Ben:

Ben

a rocking horse,
    drawn to and fro by instability;
a detour sign,
    causing undesirable journeys;
a sweeper,

> hoovering over mixed emotions;
> a coconut,
>   breaking apart piece by piece;
> a dog,
>   obeying the master;
> a trapezoid,
>   with too many angles and sides.

Though most of the students chose one of the three young protagonists as the subject of their poem, a few responded to the adult
characters in the novel. One group created an image of General
Marchand as they saw him:

Ben's Father

a GI Joe general . . . ignoring his son's deaf child sign
a phone connecting the world but unable to connect with himself
a knowledgeable jackass
reclusive burning tequila worm
mysteriously hurricaning Ben.

About the adult terrorist Artkin, a group of four students wrote:

Artkin

Artkin
A curdled shake thick and not easily disturbed.
A stop sign
Resisting the advance of enemies.
A rotten apple
The core of his rotten gang.
A diseased mosquito
Infecting victims without compassion.
A jagged knife
Tearing and cutting the emotions and thoughts of people.
Red blood
Gushing from his victims.
An octagon
Having many sides to his personality.
A streetfighter
Locked in mortal combat.

As the students composed these poems together, they compared
their responses to the novel, thus increasing their knowledge and
reinforcing their individual interpretations. They had to bridge the
cognitive gap between the abstract and the concrete, between emotion and intellect, creating apt descriptive phrases such as "a rocking
horse, drawn to and fro by instability," and "a caution flasher, pulsing

suppressed emotions." One group cleverly created a neologism, describing Ben as "a sweeper, hoovering over mixed emotions." Most likely, these readers had not thought in depth about their reactions to this book and its characters before beginning this activity. In fact, I would venture to say that in composing their poems the students discovered some things about themselves as readers: that they could think metaphorically about literature; that they had indeed formed strong opinions about the fictional characters; and that these opinions actually helped them create their own works of literature.

Taking a cue from response theory, Marcia encouraged her ninth graders to ask their own questions about what they had read. Rather than give them a list of study questions to ponder, she asked each of them to jot down four or five questions about *After the First Death* that they would like to discuss with other members of the class. The students' questions fell into five categories: character motivation; plot; author motivation; effect on the reader; and evaluative statements about the book. Here are some of the things class members wanted to discuss:

Character Motivation

- Why did Miro kill Kate? [the most often-asked question in this category]
- What, exactly, did Miro feel for Kate?
- Why did Artkin take the first dead child and dance around with him outside the bus?
- In Part II Ben has come back spiritually in his father's mind. Why does his father want him to leave?
- Did General Marchand know his son would be hurt when he used him as a decoy?
- Why was the General willing to risk his son's life that way?
- Why is Ben so emotionally depressed?
- Why did Ben kill himself?
- When the bus stalled during her attempted escape, why did Kate open the door and let Miro in? Why didn't she try to get it started again?

Plot

- What was going on in Part II? Was Ben's father just imagining, or what?
- What exactly was "the fingers" [a torture method used by the hijackers]?

- Did Ben commit suicide?
- Was Ben dead during the whole story?
- Was the General talking to the spirit of his son?
- Did Ben attend Castleton and jump off of Brimmler's Bridge, or did he die at the hospital?
- What will become of the General?
- Where was Miro heading at the end of the novel?
- Was Artkin really Miro's father?
- Where is the terrorists' homeland?

Author Motivation

- Why does Cormier have Miro kill Kate?
- Why does Cormier choose Raymond [a child] to be killed?
- Why does the author make such a big deal about Kate's bladder?
- Why does Cormier change point of view so much?
- Why does Cormier give the book an "unfinished" ending?
- Why did everyone die in the end except Miro?
- Does this book have anything to do with Cormier s life?

Effect on the Reader

- What was it about this book that made me want to read more?
- I liked the narrative changes throughout the novel. Could we talk about those?

Evaluative Statements About the Book

- Some of the details about what Miro is thinking about Kate, etc., could have been left out. It doesn't add anything to the plot and gets pretty gross.
- I admire how the killings of the two young children were not bloody or obscene. I feel he [Cormier] could have made it so (if he wanted), but I'm glad he didn't.
- He [Cormier] portrayed the father [General Marchand] as a father of today. Proud, working, but not always correct in his actions or judgments.
- I think that Miro was really falling in love with Kate. I think Kate was falling in love with Miro, just because of his innocence and vulnerability.

- I don't think that Miro should have lived.
- I don't think that Miro should have killed Kate.

If we're sincere when we tell our students that questions are often more important than answers, we can prove our sincerity by beginning any discussion of literature with questions like these, reflecting their concerns since they arise out of their own curiosity about the work. The answers to such questions will be infinitely more interesting to them than the answers to questions teachers ask. And, lest we worry about covering everything about a book that we consider important, we may be surprised to find that the students' questions allow us to do this quite nicely. Whether young adult readers address their questions in small groups, as a class, or individually in writing, they can experience the challenge and satisfaction of exploring literature from their own perspective rather than from that of their teacher or some faraway critic.

Young Adult Literature in the Ninth Grade Honors Curriculum

Because of the erroneous perception that young adult literature is too simple to be taken seriously for advanced classroom study, many teachers shy away from including it in the curriculum. Since they are not themselves sure of the value of YA literature, they find it difficult to support its use in their classrooms. Developmental psychology, however, particularly Piagetian theory, tells us that we can process new knowledge only by relating it to what we already know—the concepts of assimilation and accommodation. This applies also to our reading: if we want young adults to read and enjoy the classics of literature, we must first ensure that they *understand* these works (without the aid of *Cliff's Notes*); in order for this understanding to occur, students must be able to connect the literature to something they already know. Enter the young adult novel.

Pairing Young Adult Literature with Classics

It's hard to predict how any group of students will react to a piece of literature, especially if that literature is touted as a classic. Often the C-word itself can provoke strongly negative reactions in student readers. But most advanced students are resigned to reading what has been labeled the best literature the world has to offer, and they usually approach the task stoically, if not enthusiastically. (A ninth grader once told me that he wanted to read *Romeo and Juliet* because he heard it had a lot of great quotes and he planned to use them to impress his friends.) Knowing this, Marcia was perplexed to find that one year the ninth graders in her advanced class had little use for *Great Expectations*, while the following year's group loved the book. Since she presented the novel in much the same way to both groups, Marcia couldn't account for the difference in response.

Sometimes even the brightest students are put off by esoteric works that bear little resemblance to the world they know. For these students and their teachers there is help in the form of books like Joan Kaywell's *Adolescent Literature as a Complement to the Classics*. This two-volume work (a third volume is on the horizon) is a collection of articles by leading teachers and scholars in the field of young adult literature. Each piece pairs one or more works of YA literature with a commonly taught classic. Volume I offers an essay that might address Marcia's experience, teaching *Great Expectations*. "Leaving Home to Come Home: The Hero's Quest in *Great Expectations* and Three Young Adult Novels," by Leila Christenbury, makes careful connections between Dickens' classic and Cynthia Rylant's *A Fine White Dust*, Gary Paulsen's *Dogsong*, and Robert Lipsyte's *The Brave*. Discussing the challenges of teaching *Great Expectations*, Christenbury shows how the connection among these three young adult novels and Dickens' classic work is the mythic theme of leaving home to find oneself.

> The concept of the hero separating from the family, the community, the tribe only to find that that group holds the key to self-knowledge is common to much literature. Focusing on that aspect of *Great Expectations* can help students understand the importance of the story of Pip and why his journey of self-knowledge must start from the village and end there, why his rejection of his origins must be transformed into an embrace of them. Any of the three young adult novels [mentioned] above would make a useful pair with Dickens' work. (125)

Volume I of *Adolescent Literature as a Complement to the Classics* contains other, equally useful articles that pair various young adult novels with classics such as *To Kill a Mockingbird*, *The Adventures of Huckleberry Finn*, *Death of a Salesman*, *The Great Gatsby*, *The Scarlet Letter*, and *Romeo and Juliet*. In Volume II we find some global connections, such as an article by Lois Stover and Connie Zitlow that encourages using young adult literature as part of a thematic unit on the "Clash of Cultures" centered on Chinua Achebe's *Things Fall Apart*, as well as Joan Kaywell's piece, "Using Young Adult Literature to Develop a Comprehensive World Literature Course Around Several Classics." Other interesting ideas discussed in Volume II include pairing Huxley's *Brave New World* with Lowry's *The Giver*, and teaching Mary Shelley's *Frankenstein* in conjunction with several YA books.

Teaching Literary Elements Through Young Adult Literature

In addition to their value as partners with the classics, young adult books can increase students' knowledge about the elements of literature, an objective commonly listed on courses of study for the ninth grade. As Barbara G. Samuels points out in her article "The Young Adult Novel as Transitional Literature,"

> Adolescent novels can be used to help secondary school students discover such literary conventions as character development, style, symbolism, or plot structure as well as to introduce students to some of the themes, settings, and ideas developed in more complex adult novels. Rather than struggle with abstract concepts of freedom and social satire in *The Adventures of Huckleberry Finn*, for example, students who encounter similar themes in the simpler novel *Sounder* or the more complex adolescent novel *The Chocolate War* are better prepared to discuss and understand Twain's genius. (30)

Samuels offers several suggestions. For example, she recommends Chris Crutcher's *Stotan!* and Katherine Lasky's *Beyond the Divide* as excellent books for the study of characterization. For examining plot structure and patterns of conflict, Samuels suggests Cynthia Voigt's *Homecoming* and *Dicey's Song*. For exploring the role that setting plays in a novel, she calls attention to Robert Cormier's *The Chocolate War*. Samuels' ideas are just the beginning for imaginative teachers who are looking for literature that challenges and satisfies their brightest students. Combining young adult literature with the kinds of response activities described throughout this book provides a strong rationale for curricular inclusion across ability levels.

Other Ways of Reading Young Adult Literature

Though most secondary English teachers use a formalist approach to teach literature, focusing on plot, character, setting, theme, etc., they are by no means limited to this method. In his book *Reading and Interpreting the Young Adult Novel*, John Noell Moore reminds us that there are many other ways to approach a work of fiction. Setting out to relieve teachers of the fear of "critical theory," he "reads" a series of young adult novels, using various approaches that illuminate the works for students. For example, Moore does a structuralist reading of

Bruce Brooks' *The Moves Make the Man*, focusing on language as sign in the novel; an archetypal reading of Gary Paulsen's *Dogsong*, centering on the journey motif; a response-centered reading of Walter Dean Myers' *Fallen Angels*, revealing his own reactions to the novel; and a feminist reading of Budge Wilson's short story, "The Leaving." The final reading is of Katherine Paterson's *Jacob Have I Loved*, in which Moore looks at the book from multiple theoretical perspectives. Throughout the book Moore emphasizes the value of reading young adult literature—indeed *all* literature—from different perspectives, and he encourages teachers to try various approaches with their students to enliven literary study. Such thoughtful readings would be especially appropriate for advanced students, who would be challenged and perhaps invigorated by the opportunity to read literature differently.

The Sociological Value of Studying Young Adult Literature

Today's young adults are immersed in a fast-paced world in which changing social mores and technological advances sweep them along in a sometimes frightening current. They seldom have the chance to discuss their fears and concerns with anyone other than friends. Young adult literature, which reflects students' lives so well, provides an opportunity for such discussion. Today, when issues like political correctness and affirmative action are under fire from conservative groups, when censorship threatens intellectual freedom, when drug and alcohol abuse are common among teens, when violence holds people hostage, many young adults are confused about the relevance of these issues to their lives. Students in advanced classes who examine societal issues through young adult literature can reap a twofold benefit. First, they become more aware of the relationship between literature and life; and second, through critical thinking about fictional events that mirror their own lives, they reach a better understanding of themselves and their place in society.

Cormier's *After the First Death*—and all of his other books, for that matter—are good examples of the challenging literature available for this kind of study. Many other young adult novels, some of which were mentioned earlier in this chapter, would work as well. Even teenage horror fiction—often maligned by teachers, parents, and librarians—can serve as the catalyst for discussing the issue of social responsibility: Should the authors of such fiction be more concerned about gratuitous violence in their books? Where does social responsibility lie: With the author? the reader? the publisher?

A good resource for teachers who are interested in learning more about which works would best suit their students and their curricula is *Books for You*, published periodically by the National Council of Teachers of English. This publication, which groups titles according to theme, provides annotated entries on the latest young adult books. Another good resource is *The ALAN Review*, the quarterly journal published by NCTE's Assembly on Literature for Adolescents, which reviews thirty-two new young adult books in each issue.

Cultural differences, too, can be explored through young adult literature. Many of America's young people are unaware of how others their age live in other cultures, and assume that everyone enjoys the freedoms that they take for granted. A novel like Linda Crew's *Children of the River*, about the experiences of a young Cambodian refugee, or nonfiction like Zlata Filipovic's *Zlata's Diary: A Child's Life in Sarajevo* can be just as effective—if not more so—in communicating cultural differences and struggles as Steinbeck's *The Pearl*, which is frequently anthologized for ninth graders. Exposure to cross-cultural literature is important for students like those in Marcia's class, who attend a suburban school with other students who are middle- to upper-middle-class and who encounter few people who differ from themselves. It is also important for students from minority cultures. As Lois Stover and Eileen Tway point out in "Cultural Diversity and the Young Adult Novel," reading culturally diverse young adult literature validates the experience of such students and increases their pride in their heritage (133).

The Psychological Value of Reading Young Adult Literature

Most of us read literature for enjoyment—whether that enjoyment comes from our escape into another world, the pleasure we take in the well-wrought word, or the sensory pleasures we associate with books. But we also read to make sense of our lives. We read to see how other people handle life's problems and what consequences result from their actions. We read to explore life without taking risks. Sometimes reading can even change our outlook on things, giving us new ways of thinking about old dilemmas. And, of course, the more the fictional characters resemble us, the better.

Traditional classroom study of literature has not attended much to "enjoyment," nor has it given much credence to reader engagement with a text. This omission may be the result of an almost exclusive study of classic literature, which few students really enjoy and fewer still can truly identify with. Young adult literature, on the other hand, has the potential for increasing students' understanding of themselves and their lives by letting them study works they enjoy—a very response-centered curricular goal. This potential exists regardless of the academic ability of the student. Sharon A. Stringer deals with this in detail in her book *The Young Adult Novel and Adolescent Psychology*, in which she examines such issues as identity development, moral dilemmas, mental illness, achievement and schooling, and relationships with family and peers in conjunction with the close study of various young adult novels. Stringer's discussion of the psychology of competition, for instance, yields intriguing examples of fictional situations that mirror real-life adolescent experience. Similarly, her examination of friendships, conformity, and the need to "belong" reveals the potential value of young adult literature to its readers, who struggle with these problems daily. Budding musicians, for example, might begin to come to terms with their talent after reading Suzanne Newton's *I Will Call It Georgie's Blues* or Bruce Brooks' *Midnight Hour Encores*. Young artists might better understand their creativity—and even their isolation—through reading about Carrie Stokes' experience in Zibby Oneal's *The Language of Goldfish*. Stringer uses multiple examples to demonstrate that reading young adult literature can take students beyond enjoyment to self-understanding, and thus provide the kind of classroom study that results in a true literary experience.

Cross-Disciplinary Understanding

Perhaps one of the most exciting reasons for studying young adult literature in the classroom is its potential for enhancing students' understanding of the world. Unfortunately, the compartmentalization of curricula has made it difficult for students to see connections among their studies, especially as they cross boundaries from the humanities to the natural sciences or from the social sciences to the performing arts. The idea of using young adult literature across the curriculum is not new, but it bears repeating in this context because of its value to advanced students, who are expected to have the critical thinking skills necessary to making cross-curricular connections. Innovative English teachers who can collaborate with colleagues from other disciplines have unlimited possibilities for enriching their students' learning through the reading of young adult literature. Coordinating a history class unit on the Revolutionary War, for example, with the reading in English class of novels such as Howard Fast's *April Morning*, Esther Forbes' *Johnny Tremain*, or James and Christopher Collier's *My Brother Sam Is Dead* can enrich and enliven the study of this historical event. Reading about the American Revolution in a textbook can be informative, but *experiencing* the war from the point of view of a fictional character their own age can make the war something students will not likely forget. This is the best of all possible learning worlds, combining the kind of efferent and aesthetic reading experience that Louise Rosenblatt talks about in *Literature as Exploration*. As students read history textbooks efferently—to gain information—they read fiction aesthetically—to actually experience the events.

A Final Thought

Sandy Asher's words, quoted at the beginning of this chapter, should give teachers pause as we make curricular decisions that will have long-term effects on our students. The "empty vessel" approach to teaching, where we attempt to pour information into students' minds, won't work if we use young adult literature as a teaching tool. Granted, the study of YA literature could be reduced to a series of exercises and questions that might discourage even the most engaged reader, but the content of the literature lends itself to tapping, as Asher says, the reader's "imagination, vision, emotion"—to encouraging readers to make their own meaning as they experience a work. Students *do* have the ability to interpret literature, but in many cases it has been taken away from them by well-meaning teachers who think of their own interpretation as primary. We must give back to our students the opportunity to interpret what they read—not an easy task, especially with advanced students who have become accustomed to listening to lectures and making teachers' ideas their own. If this change is going to happen, it will happen through the reading of young adult literature, where students have ownership of the experience. What an exciting prospect: a class full of animated students arguing about their interpretations of *After the First Death* or *The Giver*. We teachers might even learn something.

Works Cited

Achebe, C. 1991. *Things Fall Apart*. New York: Fawcett Crest.

Brooks. B. 1986. *Midnight Hour Encores*. New York: HarperCollins.

————. 1984. *The Moves Make the Man*. New York: Harper & Row.

Christenbury, L. 1993. "Leaving Home to Come Home: The Hero's Quest in *Great Expectations* and Three Young Adult Novels." In *Adolescent Literature as a Complement to the Classics*, Volume 1, ed. Joan F. Kaywell, 117–126. Norwood, MA: Christopher-Gordon.

Collier, J. L., and C. Collier. 1974. *My Brother Sam Is Dead*. New York: Scholastic.

Cormier, R. 1979. *After the First Death*. New York: Dell.

————. 1983. *The Chocolate War*. New York: Dell.

Crew, L. 1989. *Children of the River*. New York: Dell.

Crutcher, C. 1988. *Stotan!* New York: Dell.

Dickens, C. 1962. *Great Expectations*. New York: Macmillan.

Fast, H. 1962. *April Morning*. New York: Bantam.

Filipovic, Z. 1994. *Zlata's Diary: A Child's Life in Sarajevo*. New York: Viking.

Fitzgerald, F. S. 1925. *The Great Gatsby*. New York: Charles Scribner's Sons.

Forbes, E. 1970. *Johnny Tremain*. New York: Dell.

Hawthorne, N. 1983. *The Scarlet Letter*. New York: Penguin USA.

Huxley, A. 1946. *Brave New World*. New York: Penguin USA.

Kaywell, J. F. 1995. "Using Young Adult Literature to Develop a Comprehensive World Literature Course Around Several Classics." In *Adolescent Literature as a Complement to the Classics*, Volume 2, ed. Joan F. Kaywell, 111–143. Norwood, MA: Christopher-Gordon.

Lasky, K. 1986. *Beyond the Divide*. New York: Dell.

Lee, H. 1960. *To Kill a Mockingbird*. New York: Warner Books.

Lipsyte, R. 1991. *The Brave*. New York: HarperCollins.

Lowry, L. 1993. *The Giver*. New York: Dell.

Miller, A. 1949. *Death of a Salesman*. New York: Penguin.

Moore, J. N. 1996. *Reading and Interpreting the Young Adult Novel*. Portsmouth, NH: Boynton/Cook-Heinemann.

Myers, W. D. 1988. *Fallen Angels*. New York: Scholastic.

Newton, S. 1990. *I Will Call It Georgie's Blues*. New York: Puffin.

Oneal, Z. 1980. *The Language of Goldfish*. New York: Fawcett Juniper.

Paulsen, G. 1985. *Dogsong*. New York: Bradbury Press.

Rosenblatt, L. M. 1983. *Literature As Exploration*, Fourth Edition. New York: Modern Language Association.

Rylant, C. 1986. *A Fine White Dust*. New York: Bradbury Press.

Samuels, B. G. 1992. "The Young Adult Novel as Transitional Literature." In *Reading Their World: The Young Adult Novel in the Classroom*, eds. V. R. Monseau and G. M. Salvner. Portsmouth, NH: Boynton/Cook-Heinemann.

Shelley, M. 1965. *Frankenstein*. New York: Signet Classics.

Stover, L. T., and E. Tway. 1992. "Cultural Diversity and the Young Adult Novel." In *Reading Their World: The Young Adult Novel in the Classroom*, eds. V. R. Monseau and G. M. Salvner. Portsmouth, NH: Boynton/Cook-Heinemann.

Stover, L. T., and C. S. Zitlow. 1995. "Using Young Adult Literature as a Companion to World Literature: A Model Thematic Unit on the 'Clash of Cultures' Centered on *Things Fall Apart*." In *Adolescent Literature as a Complement to the Classics*, Volume 2, ed. J. F. Kaywell. Norwood, MA: Christopher-Gordon.

Stringer, S. A. 1996. *The Young Adult Novel and Adolescent Psychology*. Portsmouth, NH: Boynton/Cook-Heinemann.

Shakespeare, W. 1942. *Romeo and Juliet*. In *The Complete Plays and Poems of William Shakespeare*, eds. W. A. Neilson and C. J. Hill. Cambridge: Houghton Mifflin. Originally published in 1609.

Twain, M. 1940. *The Adventures of Huckleberry Finn*. New York: Heritage Press.

Voigt, C. 1982. *Dicey's Song*. New York: Macmillan.

———. 1981. *Homecoming*. New York: Macmillan.

Three

Voigt and Kafka; Crutcher and Camus: Responding to Young Adult Literature in the Advanced Placement Class

How can you go wrong with a classic? Choose a classic and you're safe. No need to make choices. The classics are always appropriate. If you don't get it, if your students don't get it at all, the fault is not with the classic but with the reader. Of course the Emperor is royally clad. But when was the last time you really looked?

Harry Mazer

Just the thought of including young adult literature in the advanced placement curriculum is enough to send some teachers running for their copies of *Antigone* and *Oedipus Rex*. A haven for the best and brightest students, the AP class is designed to provide work that is more intellectually rigorous and challenging than that required in the conventional English class, and to give advanced high school students the opportunity to gain college credit through examination. The AP Literature and Composition Test is designed around the traditional canon, which predetermines to a great extent the advanced placement English curriculum in most schools. A look at the syllabus of one AP 12 English class is telling.

Texts: DiYanni, Robert, ed. *Literature: Reading Fiction, Poetry, Drama, and the Essay.*

Mack, Maynard et al., eds. *Continental Edition of World Masterpieces,*
2 volumes.
Supplementary Reading Material (by theme):

I. Man and His Society

1984	*Candide*	*Tartuffe*
No Exit	*Brave New World*	*One Day in the Life of*
All the King's Men		*Ivan Denisovich*

II. Man's Greatest Friend and Enemy: Himself

Zoo Story	*Metamorphosis*	*Sons and Lovers*
Daisy Miller	*Heart of Darkness*	*The Heart Is a Lonely*
The Runner	*Death in Venice*	*Hunter*
		The Wild Duck

III. The Tragic Hero

Agamemnon	*Oedipus Rex*	*Death of a Salesman*
Antigone	*Medea*	*Hamlet*
King Lear	*Saint Joan*	*Beloved*

IV. Man's Search for God and Ideals

Our Town	*The Power and the*	*A Man for All Seasons*
Waiting for Godot	*Glory*	*A Farewell to Arms*
	The Stranger	*20,000 Leagues*
		Under the Sea

Though the sexist nature of the unit titles and the weak presence of
female authors is quite disturbing, astute readers will notice a departure from the list of classic titles in Section II, "Man's Greatest Friend
and Enemy: Himself"—namely, the inclusion of Cynthia Voigt's *The
Runner,* which is commonly classified as a young adult novel. Given
the goals of the class and the nature of the advanced placement exam,
how did this novel make the list? What value might it have to students studying the "great works" of literature?

  In examining this question, I think it would be useful to mention
what some high school and college teachers have observed about
advanced placement English, then to juxtapose their views with
actual scenes from advanced placement classrooms. In his essay "The
Theory of AP English: A Critique," David Foster points out that the
guidelines for the AP Literature and Composition Course focuses
largely on objective analysis of the literary text, rooted in the New
Critical approach. Foster goes on to say:

> It is this rigid interpretive process that is the biggest pedagogical failure of the AP exam [because it] carries with it two major difficulties. One is the dilemma it poses for students responding to lexically precise questions about frequently ambiguous literary language. . . . Another problem is the exam's exclusive focus on the text, leaving individual readers' responses wholly out of account. (15)

Citing the increased pedagogical emphasis in college classrooms on the process of responding to a text, Foster charges that "the absence of concern for the reader's role in interpretation marks the biggest departure of the AP pattern from current literary theory" (18–19).

While Foster is concerned about textual objectivism in AP English, John Iorio questions the consequences of focusing AP classes solely on preparing students for the AP exam. In his essay "Preparing Students for the AP Examination: Dangers and Opportunities," he charges that "teaching for the test is reductive, self-defeating, and ultimately a betrayal of educational integrity and student development" (143). Iorio offers a series of questions that might be asked as schools look more closely at literature courses.

> Are the works being chosen by the faculty with honest conviction about what constitutes a college education in our complex civilization? Are they chosen with the intent of enlarging a student's vision? Are they chosen to stimulate modes of thinking not familiar to the student? Are they chosen to present the past not in slavish reverence but as a dynamic living presence? Or are they chosen with both eyes on the test? (147)

Both Foster and Iorio focus on the pedagogical implications of the advanced placement course, with Foster emphasizing concern for the reader over the text—a roundabout endorsement of literature that engages the student. But the thought of this literature being of the "young adult" variety may be too radical for even a critic like Foster to entertain.

Elizabeth, the AP teacher who designed the reading list above, *did* entertain such a thought: she saw *The Runner* as a novel that would help her students better understand literature by authors such as Kafka and Conrad. Herself a fan of Cynthia Voigt's work, Elizabeth saw its potential value to her students and was willing to depart from the norm in her AP classroom. After reading the novels in the unit on "Man's Greatest Friend and Enemy: Himself," Elizabeth asked the students to write a response paper that answered the question: "If you could choose one character to go out and spend some time with, who would it be and why?" Though most of the students chose characters from the classic works, a third of them chose Bullet Tillerman from *The Runner* as their preferred companion. "I liked the fact that Bullet's father told him to go get a haircut, and Bullet went and shaved it all off," wrote Chuck. He added, "I would ask him how he had the guts to purposely fix the barn door incorrectly, knowing that his father would be mad. I have often thought of doing things like that, but I just don't seem to have the guts to do it." Another student, Greg, wrote:

> I find myself wanting to know why Bullet is thinking as he is. . . . I'd ask him why he's not very interested in girls, why he's so indifferent to things, how he felt when he killed his sister's dog, why he doesn't look for his older siblings, why he runs, why he is prejudiced, what he thinks about. . . .

The students who chose Bullet as their companion apparently did so because he reminded them of themselves in some way, or because they felt that he could somehow help them understand themselves a little better in a way characters from the classic works could not. Their choice supports the contention of G. Melvin Hipps, who in his article "Adolescent Literature: Once More to the Defense" reminds us of a timeless truth:

> What we often forget is that bright students are not necessarily more advanced socially or emotionally than other students their age. . . . We also forget sometimes that conflicts that seem trivial or inconsequential to us are of earth-shaking importance to young people. Bright students, who may have more capacity for enjoying subtle vicarious experiences than slow ones do, may still have great difficulty becoming involved with the aging, impotent, cynical characters of Hemingway or Fitzgerald. (46–47)

In addition to the enjoyment we derive from our love of story, we also read literature to help make sense of our lives, yet we may be depriving our brightest students of this kind of beneficial literary experience in the classroom if we insist that they limit themselves to objective analysis of "great literature of the past."

Willing to experiment further, Elizabeth asked her AP students to read Cormier's *After the First Death* as part of their unit on "The Tragic Hero." This laid the groundwork for comparing the responses of Elizabeth's, Jean's, and Marcia's students. The discussion in Elizabeth's class focused on whether or not the novel is indeed a tragedy and, if it is, why. Sitting in a circle with Elizabeth and me, the students approached the book with the same degree of seriousness they gave to the other works they had read. The reasons they gave for considering *After the First Death* a tragedy included:

1. most of the main characters die
2. adults made erroneous choices in regard to their children
3. the young adults in the story were manipulated by their elders

4. trust was betrayed

5. young people had no control over their lives

To validate this last bit of reasoning, Tessa, who was particularly upset about the death of five-year-old Raymond in the book, replied, "They [the children] were just all so helpless and that's why I think it's tragic." But Grant quickly disagreed, prompting this exchange:

Grant: But when God takes away innocent children and they die, no one thinks that's a tragedy, but they lack control of their lives. I don't think tragedy can be defined by helplessness or lack of control.

Elizabeth: How do you feel when someone dies? Is that tragedy?

Grant: That's life. Everyone dies.

Elizabeth: Then why is death a tragedy?

Patricia: I'm not sure I think it *is* a tragedy, but I think some people might regard it that way because of their *own* personal loss, not because of the loss of the individual who actually died.

Tessa: It wasn't a tragedy for the terrorists because they didn't have any feelings for the people who died.

Colleen: Does tragedy depend on who you think the protagonist and antagonist are? What if it were American terrorists and they were holding other people to promote their cause? Would we think that was patriotism? I think we'd consider it more patriotism than tragedy.

Tessa: We consider it tragedy because Miro's values are so different from ours.

Elizabeth: So he's patriotic to his cause?

Patricia: None of us would go that far for our cause—and I don't know if it's because we're not as dedicated as he is—but the way he was taught was that's what he should fight for and that's the way he should live. So he thinks he's doing nothing wrong. The only reason we think it's tragic is because he's affecting other people we can empathize with more than we can empathize with him.

Colleen: I think Miro is tragic because we sympathize that he was brought up with that value system—being indifferent to other people's feelings. I think it's tragic, but to them it's not a tragedy. So again it comes out to relativity for each person.

As these students struggled with this concept, they came to some important conclusions about the nature of tragedy—that it's relative, that it's difficult to define specifically. Equally significant is that this young adult novel provided the depth of meaning necessary for this kind of discussion. Also interesting is the students' choice of "hero" in their discussion of tragedy. In the classics they were reading as part of this unit—*Antigone, Hamlet, Saint Joan,* and others—the protagonist/hero is one clearly defined person who readers can identify as the central character in the story. *After the First Death*, however, presents three protagonists, each of whom attracts reader allegiance for different reasons. Kate's life is in danger from the very first moment of the hijacking. She worries about her bravery, or lack of it. She becomes introspective about her life, regretting her shallowness. She risks her life to perform a heroic act. Ben's life is in danger, too, but he is too trusting of his father to realize it. He is the quintessential "good son," eager to please, eager to help—until his father betrays him. And then there's Miro, a young man who has known only violence and death all his life, who has been trained by adult terrorists to kill or be killed. He likes Elvis Presley. He's simultaneously attracted to and repulsed by things American. He doesn't know what to make of his attraction to Kate. And he kills her in a moment of emotional terror. Yet Miro is the one the students choose to talk about, the one whom they try to understand.

Elizabeth's students, like the ninth graders in Jean's and Marcia's classes, responded to a characteristic that Cormier intentionally gave Miro: an innocence that seems to transcend his angry, aggressive behavior and violent ways. Though he is a monster of sorts, Miro is also a vulnerable young man seeking his identity. Unable to even remember his parents, he recalls only a brother who was killed in an earlier terrorist attack. He has had no role model but Artkin, the adult terrorist who has trained him so well. But Cormier lets readers see the part of himself Miro has learned to suppress, his natural adolescent desires and inclinations. Miro is an enigma, and young adult readers are attracted to him. For advanced placement students he presents both an intellectual and an emotional challenge, as they label him a "tragic hero."

Later in the year, another young adult hero captured the attention of Elizabeth's students, though for a different reason. After reading *The Runner* and *After the First Death*, they read Chris Crutcher's *Running Loose* in conjunction with Albert Camus' *The Stranger* as part of their unit on "Man's Search for God and Ideals." In Crutcher's novel the protagonist, Louie Banks, must deal with the sudden death of his girlfriend, Becky, just as Meursault must deal with his mother's death in *The Stranger*. This unit was taught by Elizabeth's student teacher, Rhonda, who engaged the class in a discussion that focused on Louie's irreverent outburst at Becky's funeral, in which he accuses the out-of-town minister who delivers the eulogy of being a hypocrite because he did not know Becky. The discussion called into question Louie's relationship with God.

Rhonda: What does that outburst say about Louie, if we connect it to yesterday's discussion of *The Stranger*? We know that Meursault decided that everybody's death is the same. When somebody dies, we go on. There's nothing special associated with death. So what does that say about Louie and his views, if he wants Becky to be treated special because she died?

Mark: Well, Becky was Louie's girlfriend, and he was a lot closer to her than Meursault was to his mother.

Karina: He seems to be looking for answers because there was one point when he says he can just visualize people saying that God works in strange and mysterious ways. He sits there and [addressing his remarks to God] he says, "I'm not moving until you give me an answer. Why? And I don't want any of this 'strange and mysterious ways' stuff!" And then, on page 136, when he's at the funeral, he comments [reads] "He shouldn't have used the 'strange and mysterious ways' defense. I could have held it together if he hadn't said that." Then he starts into his tantrum, yelling at the minister.

Rhonda: So if we're going to prove or disprove that Louie is an existentialist, we know that he believes in some inner God or some cosmic purpose . . .

Mark: He says right after that, "He sits up there on his fat butt and lets guys like you earn a living making excuses for all the rotten things that happen, or maybe he does something low-down every once in a while so he can get a bunch of us together scattered on our knees." So he's really doubting what he believes at that point.

Karina: I think it's just natural, though. It seemed like his one high point in his life was Becky, and that was gone. So I think that just naturally he was going to be very upset, probably hurt *and* angry, and he was probably looking to take that anger out on whoever he could. So I think that what he says up there, part of it's probably his emotions speaking, not really his thought.

Rhonda: If we take that as the point in the book where we see some type of change—whether he said it out of passion or whether he said it because he actually believed it—from then on, where do Louie's views go? He says, "Up until that day I felt like I had a pretty good relationship with Him." Meaning God. And then, after that, where does it go? After his talks with Dakota, where do his beliefs go? Does he reconcile anything?

Mark: He sort of learns to depend . . . does it for himself more. You know, he ran for himself and didn't do it for the coach or the other kids on the team. He just did it because that was what *he* needed to do. He found something for himself.

The students obviously wanted to give Louie the benefit of the doubt, trying to justify his anger at God, seeing it not necessarily as existential alienation, but as a natural outgrowth of his sorrow and frustration at Becky's untimely death. The situation does invite this kind of exploration, and Crutcher has created in Louie a protagonist who is justified in questioning the seeming absurdity of life and the very existence of a God who would let such things happen. The students believed that age was also an important factor here, as they compared Meursault's and Louie's views of death.

Rhonda: What does Meursault believe about death at the end of *The Stranger*?

Mark: It's on page 152, "What difference could they make to me, the deaths of others?" Everyone ends up dying, so I think he realizes that.

Phil: Yeah, and this one, on page 114, he says, "We're all going to die. It's obvious that when and how don't matter."

Rhonda: So, when Meursault says something to the effect that "I've lived my life this way, and if I'd liked, I could have lived it another way," how is that different from Louie's view of life? Does he seem to have more of a . . . searching for the right way to live than Louie?

Karina: But doesn't Louie say that you can change your life while you're living it? I mean, he was living one way at the beginning when he was sort of following the football team and doing everything that Lednecky [the coach] said, and then he turns and decides after Becky dies that he's going to go out and run for himself. You said that Meursault said that he *could* live his life a different way if we wanted to. Louie sort of realizes that he *can* do that and does it while he's still alive and has the opportunity.

Mark: It seems to me that's almost a maturation period. I mean, you have to look at the ages. There's no telling what the age . . . we never get any clue as to how old Meursault is, do we?

Elizabeth: Obviously somebody who has yet to get married, who is fairly young, but whose mother is old enough to have died, so I'd put him in his thirties.

Mark: And then you have a high school senior. As an adolescent myself, I see . . . I don't necessarily feel this way, but I see a lot of people feeling like they have to do certain things to fit in, and they have to have a place in the high school. And so, I think you see Louie at the beginning doing a lot of things, partly because he enjoys them, but he doesn't really want to, but the real reason is because he wants to fit in. I think with Meursault, he doesn't have to worry about that. I mean, society's so big, there's absolutely no way you can fit into it for everybody. You're always going to do something that somebody's not going to like, so therefore he says, "I'm going to live the way I want to live." I think it's hard to compare the two because they're just too different. They're in such different situations.

Rhonda: Well, does Louie end up being more *like* Meursault at the end of the book than he was at the beginning?

Mark: I don't think he cares about fitting in that much. I mean, he was on the team, but he has the strength to separate from the team when it's not doing what he wants. Also, this is the first death that he's encountered, and Meursault, being in his thirties, he's encountered death before.

Were the students making excuses for Louie? I don't think so. They simply recognized in him what they saw in themselves: an impulsive rebellion that sometimes overtakes reason, a desire to fit in at the cost of individuality. Though they felt it was difficult to compare Louie to

Meursault because of their different situations, the students had actually come to an important discovery; namely, that we all react differently to similar situations, depending on our age, our emotional
makeup, and our prior experience. Meursault's unemotional response
to his mother's death contrasts sharply with Louie's reaction to Becky's
passing because the two are of different ages and mindsets. Some questions that might have arisen in the class discussion, but didn't, are: Do
teenagers make good existentialists? Can they, by virtue of their age,
emotional makeup, and limited experience, really embrace the existential philosophy? Is such a philosophy innate, or does it develop as a
consequence of life experience? A final, more provocative, query might
be, Is *Running Loose* any less valuable than *The Stranger* as a means of
exploring such questions?

In her article "YA Novels in the AP Classroom: Crutcher Meets
Camus," Patricia Spencer justifies classroom use of books such as
Running Loose.

> Discovering the existential elements and heroes in modern adoles-
> cent literature has been a needed addition to an advanced-placement
> English course. Naturally, the "classics" are not abandoned (Meur-
> sault goes on trial annually), but now the unit has the vitality of
> teenage existentialists who, even in the last quarter of the twentieth
> century, are searching for individuality and identity, who pose ques-
> tions, find conundrums, and validate insecurities casually disguised
> by designer jeans, lip gloss, or football jerseys. (44–45)

Citing Sartre's contention that "man can count on no one but himself," Spencer concludes: "If the purpose of a unit on philosophy in
literature is to ask students to think more deeply about life, death, and
their place in the universe, this [young adult literature] succeeds: per-
functory discussions dissipate" (46).

The truth of this conclusion was evident as the students in Elizabeth's class continued to discuss the role society plays in the lives of
Meursault and Louie Banks, and the effect of first-person narrative on
the reader.

Rhonda: Let's go back to what you said about fitting in with society. What
does Dakota tell Louie about his views? Do you remember the discussion they
had when Dakota said something to the effect of, "Look what they've done to
you here. First they had you convinced that you had to be a football star, and
now that you don't have that, they have you convinced that you need to play
this game to graduate." What is Dakota saying about society and the power it
has over Louie?

Mark: That he's letting it control his life. He's letting them set his goals rather
than setting them himself.

Elizabeth: Well, society does this. It controls Meursault, too.

Rhonda: So are Meursault and Louie trying to escape society, learn how to play by society's rules, or what?

Mark: With Meursault, I got a complete feeling of indifference. To me, he just seemed like he didn't care. He didn't hate society; he didn't love society. He didn't like it; he didn't dislike it. He just didn't care. He was there to live his life the way he wanted to.

Elizabeth: Ah, but still there's a moment of epiphany when he says, "I suddenly realized that I was guilty"—you know, the fact that society determines guilt, and that in fact he was guilty for what he had done, though he himself did not feel particularly guilty.

Rhonda: In accordance with that, I want to go back to what you said before, giving the idea that Meursault just didn't care. You feel that way probably because we're getting through Meursault's narrative the idea that he doesn't care. What do you do with Louie narrating this book? How does his first-person narrative affect you in the way that you feel about his views and how he feels about life?

Mark: By reading it through his point of view, you're reading a more positive view of the way *he* sees things than maybe you would if you read it from the principal, Jasper. If you read it from *his* point of view, you may see the things that Louie does as totally different. You probably would. You definitely would. I mean, he sees Louie as this rebellious young kid who's causing so many problems . . . but yet when you see it through Louie, you see his thoughts and you see his reasoning behind it.

Rhonda: So you tend to identify more with Louie. Earlier we asked, "Do you think Meursault should be condemned to death?" There were some yeses and some nos because we weren't quite sure whether he was guilty in our eyes because it was through his narrative. Is it the same way in *Running Loose*, where we decide that Louie is actually doing these despicable acts . . . that we can now see the reasoning because it's through his eyes? Do we tend to identify more with Louie and say, "Well, he's not a bad kid after all?" If Louie were in this high school, and he did those things, how would you feel about him, provided you didn't have this reasoning behind it?

Karina: If I knew he was her boyfriend, I wouldn't care because he has more right to act on his feelings than anyone else.

Rhonda: So you tend to believe Louie?

Phil: I think you believe him because he doesn't tell you braggingly. I mean, he says a lot of things just in the course of telling the story. He doesn't come right out and say, "Oh, I'm this great football star and I'm wonderful." He just tells you what happened to him.

Mark: He also says, "I've done really stupid things before." He's not trying to make himself look really, really good.

Phil: Plus, you do see him lying. He admits it.

Obviously these students had faith in Louie's credibility, even though he doesn't always tell the truth, as when he and his father conspire to lie to Louie's mother about his going to the cabin with Becky—a real sticking point for some adult readers. The students seemed completely sympathetic to Louie's situation and chose to overlook what adult readers might see as reprehensible behavior. In spite of his flaws, Louie is engaging, sincere, and morally courageous, and these young adults seemed more inclined to justify his questionable behavior simply because they shared his mindset. As one student said, "He has more right to act on his feelings than anyone else." The students knew that Louie is a good kid struggling with some of life's toughest lessons, and they were closer to him in experience than any adult trying to remember what it felt like to be seventeen.

For these students, exploring the possibility that Louie Banks is an existentialist was a thought-provoking endeavor made all the more intriguing by the immediacy of his plight. Though Meursault is farther removed from the students' experience, Louie can help bring Meursault closer, increasing the students' understanding of both characters and perhaps sharpening the concept of existentialism for them as well.

Reading young adult literature in the advanced placement classroom is certainly not widespread. Indeed, some teachers see it as a waste of time, labeling it "subliterature." Student responses are mixed. Responding to my questionnaire, almost all the AP students I surveyed felt that *The Runner*, *After the First Death*, and *Running Loose* fit thematically with other works they were reading, and that they considered the books well written. They believed that young adult novels of this caliber worked well in their class to balance the classical literature they were reading and to help them better understand the more difficult works. A few of the students, however, felt they were being shortchanged. They saw young adult literature as too simple for an AP class, where they expected to study the "great works" of literature. Interesting to me, but not surprising, was the students' response to my question, "Would you ever use a young adult novel as supporting evidence on an AP exam?" Most replied that they would not, citing reasons such as, "The reader of the exam may not be familiar with the work," or "The reader may have a negative opinion of young adult literature." To these AP students, audience was all, and receiving a four or five on the AP exam was their goal.

The issue of labeling cannot be ignored here. If works like *After the First Death* and *Running Loose* were not categorized as "young adult," might teachers and students react to them differently? It is most frustrating that this labeling, instituted by publishers for marketing purposes, has so profoundly influenced the lack of acceptance of young adult literature into the curriculum. But publishing is a business—and marketing strategies are not likely to change any time soon (though it would be interesting to market a book like *After the First Death* as plain old "fiction" and see what happens). Until such changes take place, the responsibility lies with teachers, who must examine their assumptions about the young people they teach and the literature those young people read.

On a final questionnaire, I asked the AP students in Elizabeth's class, "Of all the works you've read this year, which is most significant to you personally? Which is most significant academically? Eight out of the twenty-four students who responded listed *Running Loose* as the most significant to them personally. One student commented, "I liked Louie's actions in defending what he believes in. He knew when not to be tolerant. This book presented two people choosing not to have sex, and that was a positive reinforcement for readers." Another wrote, "This is one of the best books I've read this year, and I completely sympathize and identify with the main character. I found the book enjoyable *and* thought-provoking." One student, the only one who chose a young adult novel as the most significant academically, said, "*Running Loose* is most significant to me, both personally and academically, because it captures the best of both worlds. It is a very well written book that is also very much in touch with the emotional side of adolescent life."

Given these responses, it seems foolish to ignore the potential value of young adult literature to the expectations of the AP Literature and Composition Course, as stated by Jan Guffin. Guffin quotes from *The College Board Examinations in English Language Skills and Literature*:

> The AP Examination in Literature and Composition assumes the student's deliberate and systematic preparation in college-level English. In addition to being skilled in reading and analyzing literature, students should have experience in writing not only expository essays but also critical essays related to literary topics. It is assumed that students have learned to use varying modes of discourse and are able to recognize the assumptions and effects of various rhetorical strategies. Students are expected to have studied intensively a few representative works of recognized literary merit from several genres and periods. (97)

As stated here, the intent of AP English preparation seems to be to give students the ability to respond to literature "of recognized literary merit" as college sophomores would. For clarification we might ask, "Recognized by whom?" and "What constitutes 'literary merit'?" Decisions about what literature is included in a body of "great works" are political, and in making them, intellectual snobbery should not take precedence over common sense. Surely the best of young adult literature can coexist with the classics in curricula studying universal themes, modes of discourse, and rhetorical strategies. In my own university, several faculty members use young adult fiction in their sophomore literature classes. It's time for us educators to reexamine our attitudes—and to take another look at what the world of literature is producing. Who *says* that only works of the past have literary merit? Who *says* that our brightest high school students must be deprived of studying literature that is meaningful to them? Unfortunately, our students have bought into the fallacies that dictate the content of advanced placement work. The students' goal is success, and they will read what we want them to read, write what we want them to write, and say what we want them to say in order to achieve that goal. Though the AP test makers say that students may use *any* work (including young adult literature) in responding to the open question that always appears on the test, AP students are still wary. We will surely have made progress when students feel secure writing about a thought-provoking young adult novel that aptly addresses a question on an AP exam.

Works Cited

Camus, A. [1942] 1989. *The Stranger*. New York: Vintage.

Cormier, R. 1979. *After the First Death*. New York: Dell.

Crutcher, C. 1983. *Running Loose*. New York: Dell.

Foster, D. 1989. "The Theory of AP English: A Critique." In *Advanced Placement English: Theory, Politics, and Pedagogy*, eds. G. A. Olson, E. Metzger, and E. A. Jones, 3–24. Portsmouth, NH: Boynton/Cook-Heinemann.

Guffin, J. 1989. "The AP Literature and Composition Course." In *Advanced Placement English: Theory, Politics, and Pedagogy*, eds. G.A. Olson, E. Metzger, and E.A. Jones, 96–115. Portsmouth, NH: Boynton/Cook-Heinemann.

Hipps. G. M. 1973. "Adolescent Literature: Once More to the Defense." *Virginia English Bulletin* 23 (Spring): 44–50.

Iorio, J. 1989. "Preparing Students for the AP Examination: Dangers and Opportunities." In *Advanced Placement English: Theory, Politics, and Pedagogy*, eds. G. A. Olson, E. Metzger, and E. A. Jones, 142–149. Portsmouth, NH: Boynton/Cook-Heinemann.

Spencer, P. 1989. "YA Novels in the AP Classroom: Crutcher Meets Camus." *English Journal* 78.7: 44–46.

Voigt, C. 1985. *The Runner*. New York: Scholastic.

Four

"Why Can't We Do This in English Class?": Collaborative Response at the English Festival

At their finest, young adult books provide reading experiences kids never forget, moments they make their own. Imagine that.
                                                                    Sue Ellen Bridgers

So far we've seen how young adult literature can evoke response in the classroom, where students work under the watchful eye of their teacher. Students' reaction to literature read outside of the classroom can be equally enlightening. Having been involved in planning and implementing the Youngstown State University English Festival for the past ten years, I've had the opportunity to observe thousands of twelve- to eighteen-year-olds from hundreds of schools encounter numerous young adult novels on neutral ground—the Youngstown State University campus. What happens each spring as these young people come to our festival is truly an example of reader response in action and may give us some ideas for enhancing the study of literature in our classrooms.

English Festival Goals

For seventeen years the English Festival has encouraged reading and writing about young adult literature. Each April, approximately 2,400 junior high and high school students come to campus over a three-day period to participate in a variety of activities designed to elicit their response to the seven works on that year's booklist. Each student must have read all the books in order to attend, and teachers are asked to make sure their students do the reading. The festival is committed to the continued development of student literacy, and teachers are encouraged to bring *any* student who shows an interest in reading and writing, not just the "best and brightest." Festival organizers choose young adult literature as our reading material because we want to communicate to students the joy of reading and the excitement that comes with vicarious experience. Because we don't want them to associate their festival reading with classroom study, we're careful to select books that are not being taught in the schools, books that the students most likely haven't encountered before. As the festival's information brochure points out, the book selections reflect our desire to impress upon students that literature is not merely composed of works from the past, but that it is being created now. The festival is dedicated to the philosophy that reading should be a pleasure, not a chore, and the response activities we've created reflect this belief.

Insights Sessions

The Insights sessions are designed to enrich the students' experience with the festival books by encouraging them to participate in discussions, role-playing, group work, and any number of other engaging activities. Most of these sessions involve collaboration among the students, allowing them to work with people from schools other than their own. Insights sessions are staffed by people from the university, the schools, and the community, each of whom has read at least one of the young adult books on the festival list. We encourage faculty members from departments other than English to participate, and we have had people from the history department, the business school, the music school, and the psychology department serve as Insights session leaders. Community participants have included physicians, journalists, teachers, librarians, and both blue-collar and white-collar employees of area businesses—some of them parents of participating students. Session leaders are free to design their own activities as long as they focus on at least one of the festival books, and some of the activities they've designed have been quite innovative.

Alan, a junior high teacher, decided that he wanted the students in his group to think about first impressions and how they color our reading. To open the door to discussion about first impressions, he dressed as a custodian and situated himself in the meeting room before the students arrived. As they entered, they found Alan cleaning the room, seemingly unaware that a session was to take place there. Alan greeted the students as he cleaned, making small talk about why they were there and what they planned to do. After leaving the room and closing the door behind him, he quickly doffed his disguise and reentered dressed in shirt and tie, ready to be the session leader. Puzzled at first, the students gradually realized what Alan had done. He questioned them about their initial thoughts upon entering the room and about any conclusions they had drawn about the "custodian." The students confessed that they had found the man strange at first, and hadn't taken him seriously because of his dress and occupation. When the "teacher" entered the room, though, they paid attention and treated him with respect.

After a brief discussion about stereotypes and personal biases, Alan divided the students into groups and asked them to think about the characters from one of the festival books. What were their first impressions of these characters? How did these impressions influence their reading of the book? What were their impressions at the end of the novel? If their attitude toward the characters changed from beginning to end, why did this happen? Giving each group two large sheets of posterboard and some colored pencils, Alan asked them to draw their impressions of the characters as they saw them initially and as they saw them ultimately—a visual comparison of their interpretations.

One group chose Rose Lee Jefferson from Carolyn Meyer's novel *White Lilacs* as its subject. The "before" drawing shows Rose Lee as the students saw her when the white residents of her community decide to raze Freedomtown, where she and the other black characters live, and replace it with a city park. Rose Lee is a thin figure, arms outstretched, hair disheveled, tears streaming down her cheeks. Scattered throughout the drawing are adjectives describing Rose Lee as she was then: sad, afraid, quiet, unhappy, shy (Figure 4–1).

In contrast, the "after" drawing shows Rose Lee as the students saw her later in the story, after she "preserves" Freedomtown by making sketches of all its buildings before they are torn down. Now she is powerful, arm muscles flexed, legs sturdy, feet firmly planted on the ground. This time the adjectives are positive: proud, big, hefty, strong, happy, joyful, nice, helpful, useful. In the lower right corner of the drawing the students included a white lilac, representative of the lilac bush Rose Lee inherited from her beloved grandfather and nurtured most of her life (Figure 4–2).

Figure 4-1

These young adult readers felt sorry for Rose Lee at first, viewing her as a victim. Sympathetic to her plight, they wanted someone to help her. Gradually, though, they began to see Rose Lee's strength, manifested through her artistic talent, and they realized that she was perfectly capable of helping herself. Though she couldn't prevent the white residents from razing Freedomtown, she could take the advice of her art teacher and use her talent to preserve its history.

Figure 4–2

Meyer's novel is a fictionalized account of what occured in the African American community of Quakertown, near Denton, Texas, in 1921. The book obviously had an effect on this group of students, since they chose it as their focus. By encouraging them to think about reader impressions and to represent those impressions graphically, Alan engaged these young adult readers in collaborative character study, using their perceptions as a starting point to discover how and why characters change and what effect such changes can have on readers.

Two graduate students who led an Insights session took a different approach. They asked a group of junior high students to role-play a hypothetical situation in which several characters from different books meet on a wilderness hike at summer camp. Taking on the personas of protagonists from novels such as John Christopher's *The White Mountains* and Ouida Sebestyen's *Words by Heart,* the students created the dialogue that might occur if the group's adult leader were seriously hurt in a fall and lay unconscious, unable to lead them back to camp. The session leaders hung large signs around the students' necks to identify the character played by each, and gave the students some time to discuss their situation. The students then extemporaneously acted out a scene in which they remained true to their characters' personalities. The results were amazing. The students—all from different schools—collaborated and created a dramatic situation in which the characters argued with each other about who had the best idea for survival.

As the Insights session came to an end, one young man asked, "Why can't we do this in English class? It's fun." And the exercise in character study *was* fun—for both the students and the session leaders—but it was valuable, too. Remaining in character as they responded to the situation demanded that the students use sophisticated thinking skills and have a thorough knowledge of the characters they portrayed. If we want to encourage inference-making in our students as they respond to literature, this is an ideal way to accomplish that goal. One of the real benefits of this kind of activity is its appeal to both students, who see it as pleasurable, and teachers, who can utilize it to enhance the study of literature. Students won't soon forget characters whom they come to know so well. Later in the day some of the students could still be seen wearing their signs around their necks as they went from session to session.

Writing Games

A second type of collaborative response that students are encouraged to give at the festival is elicited through writing games, one of which I used in the classroom work with ninth graders discussed in Chapter 1. Each year we use an original simulation created by my colleague Gary Salvner and designed to evoke group response to works on the festival booklist. Alluding to Louise Rosenblatt's musical metaphor of performance in response to literature, Salvner points out in *Literature Festival* that "we must look for ways to provoke students to respond actively to their reading. While our literature classes have always sought to develop students' ability to look critically at what they read, they have not always encouraged students to be 'performers' who are free to reply honestly and imaginatively to literature, and thus to find a particular pleasure and satisfaction in what they read" (1.1).

Playmaker. Pleasure and satisfaction are the goals here, and they are achieved, first, by allowing students to work together and, second, by presenting them with an activity that elicits their response to literature while imitating a real-world situation. As they enter the room, students are assembled into groups by lottery, the only requirement being that they work with people from schools other than their own. This is done to encourage equal cooperation among participants and to foster the exchange of ideas among students who haven't yet talked together about the literature. The response simulation includes several components, so that everyone in the group has something to do during the activity. For example, in "Playmaker," students are asked to write a humorous one-act play starring characters from the festival books they have read. As a prewriting activity, group members brainstorm about five important characters from the books, recalling an important lesson about life that each character has learned. Each group member then chooses one of the five characters to role-play. The students' task is to write a one-act play about a rock star, Julio, who, grounded at an airport in the middle of his international tour, meets the five characters the group has chosen, who are grounded at the same airport. Julio begins to reflect on the events of his life, and each book character explains to him one important lesson he or she has learned. As an aid, students are given a script frame for the two-scene act, with some of the lines already penciled in. Their job is to compose the characters' speeches, thereby completing the script.

One group of junior high students chose as their cast of characters Jody Baxter, the backwoods boy from Marjorie Kinnan Rawlings' *The Yearling*; Lena Sills, the strong young protagonist from Ouida Sebestyen's *Words by Heart*; Salty Yeager, the main character in Sebestyen's *Far from Home*; Kit, the heroine of Elizabeth George Speare's *The Witch of Blackbird Pond*; and Hardy McCaslin, the practical joker, also from Sebestyen's *Far from Home*. Part of the characters' dialogue, which occured after they had been grounded for some time, was initiated by Julio:

Julio: [*Script frame*] Think they sell dill pickles here? I love dill pickles. Dill pickles and cream cheese. I live on them. [*End of script frame*]

Jody: I've never had a dill pickle. What are they like?

Hardy: I used to have a rubber pickle I'd use to play jokes.

Lena: Oh, I hope they forgave you!

Salty: Most people learn to forgive even awful mistakes.

Julio: [*Script frame*] I never thought of it that way. That's deep. [*End of script frame*]

Salty: [*Script frame*] Yeah, I think about things like that a lot. Take this other experience I had, for example. [*End of script frame*] My mother left me a note saying to go to an Inn called the "Buckley Arms" and to love a man there. But I later found out that the man was my father! I had a lot of mixed feelings at that time and for a long time I hated my father. Afterwards I realized that to love my father is what my Ma woulda wanted.

Kit: I know what you mean—at one time while staying with my aunt and uncle I thought that my uncle betrayed me.

Salty: It took a long time for me to forgive and forget.

Lena: My father was shot just 'cause he was Black, and I learned to forgive the killer—even though I didn't want to—and go on with my life.

Kit: I guess we've all been through some difficult times in our lives.

Later, as the fog lifts and the characters prepare to part company for their respective flights, Jody has one last bit of advice:

Jody: [*Script frame*] Just remember this—a lesson I learned once. [*End of script frame*] If things go bad, you've got to learn to deal with it. Like when I was little and I had to shoot my deer 'cause it kept gittin' inta our crops. Boy, you shoulda seen me! I was the sorriest critter in all of Florida!

Not the easiest task—collaborating with a group of people you've never met before to respond in fifty minutes to a simulation you're seeing for the first time. Yet the students immediately entered into the minds of the characters they chose, speaking authentically in the characters' voices and demonstrating their own engagement with the books. I am always amazed at the ability of seventh and eighth graders to think so quickly and precisely under such difficult circumstances. Imagine the potential for response in a classroom situation in which collaborators are well acquainted and time is more flexible.

Untold Story. In *Literature Festival*, Salvner describes another simulation we use. Called "Untold Story," the simulation asks students to work as investigative reporters "expand[ing] the plot of a literary work by creating a plausible 'untold story' related to one of the work's characters or incidents" (5.1). The students prewrite by brainstorming about character names and situations, then select a character and choose one of three story lines: previously unknown facts about the background of the character; something previously unknown about the character's involvement with one or more events in the work read; or something that happened to the character after the events of the work read. Students divide into pairs and choose the publication for which they will work: *The National Snoop* (the nation's leading gossip newspaper), *Personality* (the weekly magazine that reports on the lives of important people), or *New York Chronicle* (one of the country's most respected newspapers). The task is for each group to create, in the form of an article, an "untold story" that will be of interest to the readers of their publication. The article must fit the personality of the character the group has chosen. It must also include a picture, which students are encouraged to draw—perhaps one representing a photograph of their character or a scene from his/her untold story. After the story is complete, each group writes a cover memorandum to the managing editor of its publication, and submits it along with the article.

Shrink Rap. While "Playmaker" and "Untold Story" tap students' dramatic and journalistic potential, another simulation, called "Shrink Rap," capitalizes on their interest in rap music. This activity puts students in the role of a world-famous psychiatrist who, burned out from the stress of the job, decides one day to become a rap composer, since rap music deals primarily with the struggles and anxieties of life. This psychiatrist has treated many famous literary characters over the years (including those from the young adult books the students have read), and decides to use the experiences of these characters as material for the lyrics. Working in groups, the students do preliminary brainstorming to select a character or characters about whom they will write a song. They then compose lyrics and give each song an appropriate title. Finally, in a memo to Mr. David Gryphon of Gryphon Records, the psychiatrist persona requests a recording contract, persuasively describing him- or herself and his or her music. Since most of these simulations include a graphic component, the students are asked to create an advertising design that will be used to promote the psychiatrist's first rap song.

In response to this scenario, a group of four high school students composed a rap song about Rainbow Jordan—from Alice Childress' novel of the same name—called "Lies At the End of the Rainbow." The voice is that of Miss Josephine, Rainbow's foster mother.

VERSE 1:   Left alone by her mother in the night,
            She came to me with no goals in sight.
CHORUS: I tried to help her the best I could.
            Children like that are not well understood.
            They keep on hurtin', the pain never dies.
            All she knows is lies, lies, lies.
VERSE 2:   It started with her mother, who didn't want her by
               her side.
            Rainbow knew the truth, from it she wished to hide.

CHORUS

VERSE 3:   She says she's always hurtin' and the pain is very
             deep.
             Her relationship with Eljay was something she
             couldn't keep.

CHORUS

VERSE 4:   She says she's tryin' to do right by Ms. Josie's ways.
             She tries harder and harder and gets better every
             day.

CHORUS

The memo, in the voice of the psychiatrist, explains the group's
request for a recording contract:

> Upon driving in my car one day, I accidentally flipped to a rap sta-
> tion and found myself engrossed. Though I previously thought this a
> deplorable form of music, I was enlightened. I thought this could be
> a new, innovative way for me to reach young people, while entering
> a new career. The rap audience is large, but the artists often deal
> with more complex problems that kids don't encounter until they
> are much older. Therefore, I believe that my song will be attractive
> to kids for its sound and rhythm and because they can relate to the
> subject matter. It is based on my experiences with my patients. The
> song I've written is "Lies At the End of the Rainbow." It deals with
> Rainbow Jordan, who grew up in the inner city with a mother who
> abandoned her. The only person who stood by her was her foster
> mother, Miss Josephine. Ms. Jordan lost confidence in herself and
> feels she must live up to the stereotype of a young inner-city girl
> who "shuts up and puts out." This lack of self-esteem is common in
> many young girls, but especially in Ms. Jordan because no one has
> ever said they believed in her.
>   I feel that my music can reach young people and ensure the
> future of our nation. In addition, this will make money for you while
> exempting you from the problems with censors and parents. If any-
> thing, you'll receive praise for your efforts with teens.

Though the song lyrics accurately depict Rainbow Jordan's di-
lemma, the memo offers more information about her problems, giving
the reader a clue to the students' insight into the novel. They are
obviously sympathetic to Rainbow, but it's interesting that they don't
let her speak for herself. Instead, they present the situation from Miss
Josephine's point of view. If this activity had been completed in the
classroom, it might have been useful to ask the group members—four
female students—why they chose Miss Josephine as the voice for their
song. Bringing their reasons to their attention could stimulate further
thought and provocative discussion about the students' transactions

with this work of literature. Starting with their song lyrics, the discussion could further explore their perceptions of the novel's events. Who is lying to Rainbow, in the students' estimation, and with what consequences? Why does this bother them as readers? Why is Rainbow misunderstood? What, exactly, does Miss Josephine do to help her and why? How do the students see Rainbow at the end of the novel?

Activities such as this give students positive experiences with literature, valuing their responses and assuring them that they do have something to say about what they read. Working with others removes the threat of being a lone voice in a discussion and almost always proves enlightening as group members share their reactions to a work. Learning takes place as readers respond within the confines of the simulation. To be successful at simulations, the readers must thoroughly understand the work and its characters, they must be able to make inferences and form hypotheses, and they must use language effectively—all skills that teachers wish to develop in their students. But what about evaluation? In "Responding to Literature from Within," Salvner offers a caveat.

> Evaluations of gaming activities, if they occur at all, must emerge from the game's created world for the activity not to be damaged by them. In the "Untold Story," for example, the evaluator's only proper role is as editor of the publications presented in the game. In that role she might want to measure the overall quality of the writing, the appropriateness of the style for that particular publication, the newsworthiness of the untold story, and the story's consistency with facts already known about the character (as revealed in the original work of literature). (78)

Though these writing games were designed to be completed in fifty minutes at the English Festival, they are certainly applicable to the classroom, as Salvner illustrates in his book *Literature Festival*. Enterprising teachers interested in literary response will find these games challenging and creative, and students will welcome the opportunity the games give them to study literature actively.

Festivideos

One of the most creative forms of response that we encourage at the English Festival is students' creation of videos that depict some aspect of a literary work or works they have read. In the spirit of our project, we call these "Festivideos." Almost all of the videos produced have been collaborations among students from specific schools. In some cases, one or two students are the actors, and one or two work behind the scenes. For example, one group of eighth graders created a video

called "Express Yourself," in which they simulated a talk show where
a moderator was interviewing Mick, the artist in Gary Paulsen's book
The Monument. Viewers of the talk show were invited to call in with
questions. The students offstage who played the callers injected
humor into the situation by making outlandish suggestions about the
sort of monument that Mick should create for their town to memori-
alize the war dead. One suggested that Mick do something on black
velvet. When Mick politely declined, the miffed caller abruptly hung
up and we heard a dial tone. Throughout the interview, a confident
Mick sipped coffee from a mug, which he periodically placed on the
coffee table in front of him. The attractive set included comfortable
furniture and a background of wooden shelves filled with books. At
the end of the show, the moderator introduced the cast, including the
people whose voices were heard as callers.

A particularly effective video was created by a twelfth grader
around Kathryn Lasky's novel *Night Journey*, in which an old Russian
woman, Nana Sashie, now confined to her bed, tells her granddaugh-
ter Rachel of her family's escape from the Nazis, in which she played
a major role as a young girl. The student playing the role of Nana
Sashie looked remarkably in character, wearing a specially designed
mask crafted to resemble the old woman's face as it's drawn in the
book's illustrations. Sitting propped up in bed, wearing a bed jacket
around her shoulders and a babushka over her head, Nana Sashie told
her story as she displayed the drawings that depicted its important
events. Her Russian accent was amazingly authentic as the camera
alternately focused on her face and the drawings, which she picked up
periodically from the nightstand next to her bed. Nana Sashie's narration included all the important events of the book, and her body
language, especially her hand gestures, added to the video's effectiveness. She even had at her bedside a plate of cookies containing gold
coins, just like those she baked to bribe the border guards long ago.
At one point in her story Nana Sashie slipped and called the border
guards "soldiers," then chided herself for her mistake and blamed it
on her eighty-year-old mind. One of Nana Sashie's most prized pos-
sessions is her samovar, which she showed her viewers, inviting them
to come and have tea with her as she ended her story.

Also patterned after *Night Journey* was a video created by a group
of eighth-grade students who focused in a different way on the storytelling aspect of the book. They decided to go out and interview prom-
inent people in their community, inviting them to tell stories of their
own grandparents. The interviews were conducted at the offices of
these community leaders, so the sets varied from a conference room,
to a spacious office, to a reception area furnished with comfortable

sofas and chairs. The stories included memories about a grandfather who, though he had a demanding job as dean of men at a local university, always found time to take his grandson to football games; a grandmother who started a small bakery that has now become the largest in the city; and another grandmother who, coming to America as an immigrant at age sixteen, opened a grocery store in her home and eventually gave her husband his first contracting job—building new steps for her store. Today this family is internationally known for its mall development. These interviews were interspersed in the video with the students' own recollections of their grandparents, and one young woman proudly remembered her Jewish grandfather, who once acted with Orson Welles and who went to high school with Israeli prime minister Golda Meir. All of the students encouraged viewers to listen more closely to the stories grandparents tell. To underscore their point, one of the students quoted from an anonymous poet:

> Preserve your history and become everlasting.
> Receive new life from the times that have gone by.

Creating visual representations of their response to young adult literature allowed these students the kind of freedom of expression not possible in discussion or writing. By tapping their flair for the dramatic, this kind of response allows an orality that often lies hidden in students who find conventional discussion too threatening and writing too confining. Dramatic response allows more latitude for interpretation, more flexibility of choice, more liberation from the tyranny of "correctness." And yet, if we were to use these videos as a test of what the students learned, we would see that this freedom yielded as much, if not more, insight into the books as a question-and-answer quiz would have. More important, it affirmed the students' ability to interpret literature on their own.

An interesting observation here is that many of the students' responses focus on the adults in the story rather than on the young protagonists, giving us cause to question our assumptions about young adult readers. Though they most certainly identify with characters near their own age, perhaps young adult readers are paying close attention, without realizing it, to how adults in the stories live their lives. The young characters represent the here and now for the young readers, but it is the adults who give a glimpse into the future, into who or what the readers may become. They admire Mick, Miss Josephine, and Nana Sashie because these are adults who have taken charge of their lives. In their book *Literature for Today's Young Adults*, Nilsen and Donelson talk about the external locus of control ("What will happen to me?") versus the internal locus of control ("What am I going to do with my life?"):

> Although we all know adults who operate under an external locus of control . . . most of us would agree that we want to help young people develop an internal locus of control. . . . But developing an internal locus of control is not something people can do simply because they are told to, nor is it something that can be learned as a skill, such as bicycle riding or swimming. Instead it is a way of looking at life, which develops slowly over many years in such infinitely small steps as three-year-olds choosing what clothes they will wear and fifteen-year-olds choosing who their friends will be. Identifying with characters in books as they develop into maturity is another of these infinitely small steps. (44)

Response to literature does give us clues to the psychological development of young adults. Paying close attention to this response, whether in an extracurricular activity like the English Festival or in our own classrooms, can only benefit us as we try to instill a love of literature in our students—and inject new life into our teaching. In "'The Guy Who Wrote This Poem Seems to Have the Same Feelings You Have,'" Leila Christenbury makes a confession that may touch a nerve for many of us:

> I discovered reader response out of my own failure to entice my students to celebrate what I perceived to be the great craft of literature. I think I had forgotten that appreciation came to me after, sometimes long after, I had experienced how a novel or a short story could make me feel, could tell me about my life, my problems, my capabilities. (34)

Young adults love to talk to each other. Indeed, teachers expend valuable energy trying to silence students in the classroom in order to get some teaching done. Why not combine the talk and the teaching? Young adult literature is the perfect tool.

Works Cited

Christenbury, L. 1992. "'The Guy Who Wrote This Poem Seems to Have the Same Feelings You Have': Reader Response Methodology." In *Reader Response in the Classroom*, ed. N. J. Karolides, 33–44. New York: Longman.

Childress, A. 1982. *Rainbow Jordan*. New York: Avon.

Christopher, J. 1970. *The White Mountains*. New York: Macmillan.

Lasky, K. 1981. *Night Journey*. New York: Puffin.

Meyer, C. 1993. *White Lilacs*. San Diego: Harcourt Brace.

Nilsen, A. P., and K. L. Donelson. 1993. *Literature for Today's Young Adults,* 4th ed. New York: HarperCollins.

Paulsen, G. 1993. *The Monument.* New York: Dell.

Rawlings, M. K. 1970. *The Yearling.* New York: Scribners.

Rosenblatt, L. M. 1983. *Literature As Exploration,* 4th ed. New York: Modern Language Association.

Salvner, G. 1991. *Literature Festival.* Lakeside, CA: Interact.

————. 1982. "Responding to Literature from Within: The Untold Story Game." *Kentucky English Bulletin* 32.1 (Fall): 77–87.

Sebestyen, O. 1980. *Far from Home.* New York: Dell.

————. 1981. *Words by Heart.* New York: Bantam.

Speare, E. J. 1980. *The Witch of Blackbird Pond.* New York: Dell.

Five

Abolishing "Textoids": Individual Response Through Writing

Writing, being a writer, is wonderful. I love it more than anything else in the world. I think it's God's gift to me, and I would like to be remembered as giving something back to the world.
Walter Dean Myers

In his monograph *Critical Thinking and Writing: Reclaiming the Essay*, Thomas Newkirk recalls his bad memories of the school essay—the formulaic, restrictive thesis-control paper that still seems to dominate writing instruction. Quoting Jerome Harste, Newkirk labels such an essay a "textoid," totally superficial and devoid of life (4). He recommends that teachers "use writing as a tool for thinking rather than . . . a formula for how 'good essays' ought to be written" (vi). To underscore his point, Newkirk asks:

> Does the "thesis-control essay" . . . the mainstay of expository writing programs, actually limit the inquiry that writing supposedly should foster? Is the level of "preformulation" needed to produce such an essay consistent with the view that writing can help the student explore a subject? And does this requirement to formulate a thesis and "defend" it bear any resemblance to what essay writers do? . . . The curious misdirection of the thesis-control essay is suggested by the clear requirement to students that the essay be used to

"back up" the thesis. The reader is expected to move forward in a text that is continually backing up. (6–7)

Newkirk's words apply not only to the generic generate-your-own-subject essay that students are commonly asked to write, but are also significant when we consider the response-to-literature essay that teachers often assign, since our students' written response often helps shape their understanding of a text. Think about it. If after reading Robert Cormier's *The Chocolate War* we ask our students to write an essay that defends Jerry's decision not to sell the chocolates, how much exploration can they really do? Conscientious writers will most likely make an outline listing supportive reasons, then structure an essay around a thesis that these points will illuminate. Though the result may be a grammatically and structurally sound piece of writing, it most likely will have no voice because the writer will be absent. Consider the opening paragraph of this essay, the response to an assignment to write a comparison of two young adult novels.

> Society regards sharing as important; it is taught at an early age. Young children learn to share their books and toys with their fellow classmates. They learn to share and carry this concept into adulthood. Sharing is important in Cynthia Voigt's *Homecoming* and Felice Holman's *The Wild Children*. In these novels, the sharing of food and shelter, and of a variety of different feelings, occurs between the main characters, who are children. Sharing becomes a vital part of the children's new lives without parents. Without sharing, it is probable that none of the children would have survived their long, treacherous journeys.

This writer has hit upon the concept of *sharing* as the focus of his essay, and, predictably, the body of the paper lists instances of sharing that took place in each novel. Examples in the paper include one or two quotes from the books, since that was one of the requirements of the assignment, and the writer concludes with this paragraph:

> Sharing was shown to be an important part of these two novels. By sharing, Alex and the band and Dicey and the other children finally found a new world of happiness. Sharing got them through many tests of their strengths: physical, mental and emotional. These children showed an incredible power to overcome the odds and the adults who threatened them. Everyone must share to survive. Without sharing, the human race could cease to exist. Dicey knew that sharing was important when she told the younger children, "We gotta stick together" (Voigt, 31).

In the opening and closing paragraphs alone, variations of the word *share* appear thirteen times. We might ask, "Did this writer really care about the sharing that took place in these books, or did he settle on the concept as a convenient point of comparison that he could trace successfully for the assignment?" Nowhere in the essay is there any sense of connection between the reader-writer and the books' characters. Nowhere does the writer explore the characters' motivations to behave as they did. The essay is purely factual, citing instances of sharing and describing how and where they took place. It concludes with platitudes that enable the writer to exit the text with his thesis intact.

Place the preceding essay alongside the following one, written in response to a more specific prompt that asked students to write an essay comparing two young adult novels, focusing on lessons that characters learn through their fictional experiences. The opening paragraph reads:

> Often we learn our greatest lessons when we are left alone to ponder life, our existence, and our actions. "Loners" are often misunderstood and under-estimated, but "loners" usually prevail, as we witnessed Bullet in *The Runner* by Cynthia Voigt and Annie of *Captives of Time* by Malcolm Bosse.

This writer begins in much the same manner as the previous writer, setting up the essay by telling us which books she's responding to and letting us know her thesis. But beginning with the second paragraph, she puts herself into her text, and though she writes mostly in the expository, third-person mode, we get the feeling that she is talking as much about herself as she is about Bullet and Annie. She writes:

> Bullet is the ultimate or the ideal loner. He thinks for himself, he defies social "norms," and he is the master of his own decisions. This is why it is not surprising that he is a cross-country runner. Although he uses his running as periods of escape and peace (as most runners do), this does not make him a typical loner. I believe he is a logical loner, one who does not need to justify his beliefs to those who fear individuality. Bullet's strong will nurtures his ability not to give in to conformity, a characteristic all of us could use more of. . . . Many of us think, "Don't box me in, society. I want to be my own person." Bullet not only thought this, but he made sure society knew and understood every word.

Acknowledging the historical accuracy of Bosse's book, the writer moves on to discuss the character of Annie:

> The historical viewpoint in *Captives of Time* is enough to captivate any reader, but the strength of Annie's character is so unforgettable, there's no way the reader can leave unenlightened. What does it take to succeed as a loner? to maintain a sense of who we are? It takes courage . . . lots and lots of courage. This is one of the greatest factors of Annie's character: her courage to accept isolation, danger,

and loneliness. . . . Annie is an example of the loner who is also lov-
ing and caring, traits we do not expect of a loner. This is exactly
where loners are often misunderstood. Loners are also lovers—they
cry, they feel, they sympathize. To characterize a loner as someone
selfish or egotistical is one of the most common false judgments
people/society make. Annie's position as a loner gives her the
strength to defy authority and, as Bullet did, decide where, when,
and how she would take on the world.

Taking her place alongside the characters, the writer concludes:

> Annie and Bullet are not typical "loners." Actually, I do not believe
> there is a typical loner. We are all different—and we all learn from
> our experiences. We're analytical, sometimes outspoken (yet usually
> shy). We're all fighting for our souls, our survival, our own causes.
> I learned much from Annie and Bullet—their personalities as loners
> assured me of my own value and worth. When it comes to loners,
> we share a bond. Believe me, I speak from experience.

It's both exciting and frustrating to watch what happens in this essay.
The writer, obviously choosing the "loner" focus because it has personal meaning, is tentative at first about including herself in the
paper. Not until the end of her second paragraph, when she says,
"Many of us think, 'Don't box me in, society. I want to be my own
person',," does she reveal her own connection to the characters. After
that, the writer gradually creeps into the text, using the pronoun *we*
as she asks rhetorical questions about success and identity, taking
umbrage at society's view of loners. In her final paragraph she disap-
pears completely into the text.

   This writer is just getting started when the essay comes to a close.
As she worked her way through the first few paragraphs, she began
to explore the loner in herself by responding to the characters of Bullet and Annie. She almost let the assignment "box her in" but began
to wriggle free as she wrote. Without realizing it, the writer discovered that, as Newkirk says, "the evolving text will tell [her] what to
write" (15). Newkirk pinpoints it exactly when he says:

> If beginning writers never have this experience of the writing taking
> over—the emerging language outpacing the original intention, the
> digression becoming a central part of the writing—they will never
> understand what it is that motivates writers. And the essay must be
> open enough for this movement into the unknown. (16)

   What accounts for the differences in these two essays? The first
was written by a male student in ninth grade; the second, by a female
student in twelfth grade. The first was written outside of class; the
second, as an impromptu exercise within a fifty minute time con-
straint with no advance knowledge of the topic. We might say that

the first writer is less experienced and therefore more inclined to
adhere to a writing formula. We might say that the second writer has
a naturally more expressive style and a natural inclination to make
connections with the characters. We might even say that she, being
older, is less fearful of taking risks in her writing. Might we even
speculate that she, writing in an impromptu situation, felt more freedom to be herself? Though logic might say that writing a timed essay
under duress would result in a response of lesser quality than one
written in a more leisurely fashion, this writer seems to contradict
that assumption. Given the assignment, her essay could have been as
stiff and formal as the first writer's—indeed, it started out that way. I
believe that the writer succeeded in spite of the assignment, allowing
the writing to lead her, ending her piece by talking directly to her
readers—even risking the understood "you."

If we want our students to respond to literature in new and fresh
ways, we need to help them escape the bonds of the traditional essay
form. One way to accomplish this is by creating rhetorical situations
that give students an audience and purpose for writing. For example,
one assignment presented students with this rhetorical problem: You
are chair of a committee that is holding a benefit auction to which
anyone can contribute items for sale. You have asked two of the
characters from the books you've read to each donate one item that is
unique and meaningful to them. Identify these characters, explaining
their reasons for donating these particular items. In response, one
junior high student wrote:

> When I asked Jackie McGee [of Ouida Sebestyen's *The Girl in the
> Box*] and Izzy Lingard [of Cynthia Voigt's *Izzy, Willy-Nilly*] for an item
> to submit to the benefit auction, they quickly found two unique and
> meaningful items to offer me. Jackie came back the next day carry-
> ing a medium-sized cardboard box. When she lifted the lid, I peered
> over to discover a small grey touch-type typewriter. I looked at her
> curiously for some sort of explanation. Reading the expression on
> my quizzical face, she quickly began talking:
>
> > I'm donating this typewriter for important, even personal, rea-
> > sons. This little machine was my ticket to survival. When I had
> > no one to talk to, nothing to do, and nothing to see, this was the
> > only thing that kept me going. . . . It's amazing how a simple
> > tangible object that can't think, feel, or move can be a human
> > being's stimulus for life. But I've decided it's time to let go. It
> > belongs to a part of my life that I don't want to look back on
> > fondly. Once the typewriter is separate from me, I can move
> > forward with my chin up and no turning back. Besides, you
> > never know if a person will encounter a situation where a type-
> > writer will be their only companion.

Anyone can imagine that by this time I was extremely "psyched out" by Jackie's contribution. Within three days, Izzy showed up at the auction center carrying a small plastic bag. Smiling, she handed the bag to me, obviously proud of what it contained. I reached my hand into the bag and pulled out a mirror. It wasn't an antique or a flashy fluorescent color. The mirror was quite ordinary, with a plastic frame and handle. Before I even asked, Izzy gave the most beautiful speech I've ever heard:

> I know it's just a simple mirror, but it's really more than that. I want someone to look into this mirror and see who they really are, what they truly believe, and what they're ready to stand up for. It's not just a pretty face they're supposed to be looking at because their appearance isn't important. I want them to see themselves, and to do that, they must realize that no mirror can tell them what they look like on the inside or what they're feeling. . . .

It was then that it dawned on me that this auction wasn't just an event—it was part of people's lives, their history, and their future.

Because the essay prompt invites personal involvement, this writer was a part of her text from the very beginning. Though her opening sentence is pretty much a repetition of the prompt, the rest of her essay reveals her as a ventriloquist of sorts, as she uses the voices of fictional characters to communicate her own response to the characters and to the events that occured in the books. The writer obviously admires both Jackie and Izzy, giving them the characteristics of insight, maturity, and unselfishness in their selection of items to donate to the auction and in their reasons for making those selections. The writer's own insight into the novels is apparent in the speeches she has Jackie and Izzy give. And since the essay was written in fifty minutes without advance knowledge of the topic, it's safe to assume that the last sentence truly reveals a discovery on the part of the writer, reflected in the words, "It was then that it dawned on me . . ."

Lest we worry about how to evaluate essays written in response to unconventional prompts, we need only think about what this essay reveals: (1) The writer read and understood these two novels. (2) She went beyond literal plot comprehension to insightful analysis of the characters and their situations. (3) She was able to use the characters' voices to communicate her response (no easy task). (4) She wrote descriptively and fluently about the characters as she successfully situated them—and herself—in the rhetorical circumstance. (5) As a result of writing the essay, the student made a significant discovery about herself as a reader.

When we compare this essay by an eighth grade writer with the earlier piece on sharing written by a ninth grader, we see what a difference a prompt can make in the level of response to young adult literature. Allowing students the freedom to interact with characters from the fiction they read almost guarantees a more honest, lively response than that resulting from the confining thesis-control essay.

Of course, there's always the question of whether a specific prompt is even necessary to elicit a reader's response to a work. Logic would tell us that if a reader is truly engaged with a work, some form of response would come naturally. If we adults think of our own behavior after reading, we realize that usually our first inclination is to tell someone of our reaction—whether it be positive, negative, or somewhere in between. We talk about whatever we want, whatever impressed us, and we don't worry about adhering to someone else's critical guidelines. Why must it be any different for our students? I can't help but think here of a bright young woman I know, an English major, who hated to take part in book discussions in class. She even refused to talk with me in private about books we had both read. Though she wasn't aware of it at first, this student had somehow convinced herself that she had nothing interesting to say about her reading (which made her think of herself as abnormal). Years of hearing teachers tell her what she should have seen in a work assured her that literature contains hidden secrets to which only a few are privy. Only her love of language and her interest in writing kept this young woman from abandoning her major altogether, and it's not surprising that she chose professional writing as her career. To this day she describes her literature classes as the least exciting of all her English courses. It's to students like this that we owe an apology for never letting them tell us, on their own terms, what it *feels* like to experience literature.

Skeptics might say that inexperienced readers and writers need some parameters within which to work, otherwise they may digress and move away from the text altogether in their response. But to this, reader response critic Robert Probst says, "So what?" In his article "Writing from, of and about Literature," Probst validates the expressive response, giving the example of a student who, after reading John Knowles' *A Separate Peace,* wrote about his grandfather, who like Finney in the novel, also had died unexpectedly. Says Probst:

> It could be argued that his writing was not about the literature, not about *A Separate Peace,* and of course we must grant that it was not about the *text.* It did not analyze the friendship between Gene and Finny, or Gene's inability to express it; it did not discuss Knowles's

vision or style; it did not explain anything about the work itself. But it did, clearly, deal with the *reader's experience* with the text. (118–119)

Quoting Wolfgang Iser, Probst points out that "the significance of the work . . . does not lie in the meaning sealed within the text, but in the fact that that meaning brings out what had previously been sealed within us" (119). Probst uses the student writing about his grandfather as an illustration of writing "from" literature rather than "about" it, a distinction teachers would be well advised to heed.

I have learned from my undergraduate students that writing "from" literature does promote understanding, as shown in their responses to Ouida Sebestyen's *The Girl in the Box*, a novel about the abduction and captivity of sixteen-year-old Jackie McGee. I asked students what effect the novel had on them as readers and invited them to speculate on the significance of that effect. Most of the students were not far removed from their own adolescence, and their reactions were telling. One young woman wrote:

> *The Girl in the Box* was a very emotional experience for me. It seemed to touch the most sensitive parts of my life, especially relationships with my parents and friends. It also explored the pains of growing up and being hurt by friends, something I had forgotten but was startled to be so vividly reminded of. ·

Another student marveled at the novel's ability to draw her in:

> The entire time that I spent reading this novel my heart felt constricted, as if I were in shock over an event that took place before my eyes. . . . I related well to Jackie, [and] maybe that's why I was affected in such a manner. I could feel the desperation in her writing for myself with the utter, unspeakable fear of being trapped there until she dies. I believe that could be a secret fear for myself: to die alone, isolated, without any choice or way to rectify the situation.

Reflecting on the perceived invincibility of young adults, a third student wrote:

> The book helped me to realize how much most people take life for granted. We just assume that life will continue on in a normal routine, forever. . . . I realize that no matter when we die we will always have more things we wished we would have said or done.

One young woman was particularly impressed with the change that took place in the protagonist as a result of her abduction and captivity:

> I felt terrible, sad, and I wanted her to be rescued desperately. Why did this have to happen to her? I liked Jackie McGee. I respected her

because she was an honest person, very caring about herself, family and friends. . . . I reacted this way because my childhood was great up until I hit high school, then the adolescence came out and tested me every day. I feel maybe if I was "in the box" I could have put things into perspective a little better.

Comparing Jackie's situation to his, a young man in the class wrote:

I started to think how lucky I am. Here was a girl who was being held captive in a box, yet she existed with the bare necessities. I am fortunate; I have in my possession just about everything I would ever want. . . . I found out something about myself that I've never taken into serious consideration before. Sure, I care about others and what happens to them, but I have the tendency . . . to put myself first and to look out for "Number 1," me.

Some reactions were more openly hostile, however. Several students were frustrated and angry at what Sebestyen had done. Some examples:

I found myself . . . upset and "ticked off" at the conclusion of this story. I've read many books in my life, but only a handful have really moved me. *The Girl in the Box* is one of them, even though it moved me in a negative way. . . . I literally threw the book across the room once I finished it.

I really hated this book! . . . I hated witnessing the slow deterioration of this girl's mind and spirit. I feel like I was forced to see her tortured. I felt bad about myself because I wanted to help and couldn't. At many points in this book I was so revolted that I just didn't want to learn what I was learning, yet I could not put it down because, after all, we are all sucked into gruesome details.

The Girl in the Box was very unrealistic to me. I can't imagine being kept in a small dark cellar and not doing anything to find a way out. I kept asking myself why Jackie didn't try kicking the door down or finding some other means to get out. It was frustrating to see her typing away when she could have been trying to escape. . . . I can accept the fact that she was in a helpless situation, but why not at least try to do something?

Several of these examples reveal a phenomenon among some readers: a failure to appreciate the effectiveness of a book that evokes a strongly negative response. Such readers believe that they hate a book when in fact they are fascinated by its power to make them react so strongly. It's almost as if the author is writing about *them*, playing them, as Louise Rosenblatt says, like an "instrument," but striking some discordant notes along the way (279). Having the opportunity to ask questions, to vent their anger and frustration in writing, can increase students' understanding of the literary work and their reaction to it.

While we're thinking about the concept of writing "from" literature, we might also consider the poem as a form of response—an experience that Probst calls writing "of" literature. He states:

> It seems reasonable to assume that some benefit might accrue from efforts to produce, as well as receive, literary works. If we wish students to understand the structural complexities of literary forms, then efforts to create in those forms should be instructive. More important, the attempt to write literature might teach students something about the mind of the writer, helping them to see how the writer of poetry or fiction sees and thinks. (122)

With this rationale Probst departs a bit from his earlier assertion that response is valuable because it helps readers better understand themselves and others. Now he talks about response as pedagogy, focusing more on its value to achieving traditional educational goals than on its value to the reader. But I have found that poetry does offer a medium for students to express their reactions to a work of literature. For example, one high school student, responding to Cynthia Voigt's *Homecoming*, wrote this:

> Leather hands grip on
> aged wood,
> living friend
> and eternal companion.
> The grass forms endless
> rings
> and small birds trace
> them
> with infinite care
> contemplating
> the eventual
> end of
> the sun
> and the rains
> to come
> in the presence
> of aged wood.

This poem could be the writer's view of Gram Tillerman, the salty, independent woman who takes in her abandoned grandchildren, or it could be a vision of the future of thirteen-year-old Dicey, the book's protagonist—so much like Gram in her strength and determination. Or maybe it's just the writer's reflection on the mystery of life and death, prompted by the events of this novel. Whatever its meaning, to

the writer or to the reader, the poem is literature produced in
response to literature—a poem both *about* and *from* a poem. It's nice
to think that a piece of responsive creative writing such as this can
stand alone, beauty for beauty's sake, untouched by pedagogical aims
or behavioral objectives. It just *is*, like the following poem written in
response to *The Runner*, also by Cynthia Voigt:

> Carefree
> "Ha, hahahaha!" Running away. Inhaling the wind.
> To be free, to let loose and forget
> Everything—ten thousand
> Pounds on your head—is delight.
> Temporary insanity: "Who cares what I do?
> So what if I trip and fall?
> I am really flying,
> Don't want to come down, ever!
> I'm holding unexplainable happiness
> Here in my hand.
> It's golden.
> It's filling me.
> It's not real
> Except for five minutes more.
> Oh, stay!"

What might happen if we asked our students to themselves
respond to this student's poetic response, or to the response of one of
their classmates? What if we gave them a choice of forms: journal
response, short story, letter, newspaper article, song, drawing, photograph, even another poem? Such an assignment would surely tap
their creative energies, allowing them to see the work of their peers
in a different light. Any piece of writing evokes some kind of response
in the reader, and though we can respond to response ad infinitum,
it's important for our students to see that each reader is unique and
that response is not limited to one form or to works by established
writers.

Response is personal, of course, and it emerges naturally from our
transactions with anything we encounter, whether it be people, situations, or texts. Why should we keep our students from experiencing
the freedom that response can bring in the English classroom? Why
do we have to hem them in with guidelines about theses, transitions,
and conclusions when they write about what they read? The formal
essay does have its place, but not as the beginning point of response
to literature. Perhaps if the student who wrote the essay about Bullet
from *The Runner* had had the opportunity to talk with the student
who wrote the poem about the same character, she might have broken free of her constraints sooner and her writing might have been

enriched as a result. Before we can expect our students to analyze and quote we have to give them permission to hypothesize and feel. How else can we abolish "textoids"?

Works Cited

Bosse, M. 1987. *Captives of Time*. New York: Dell.

Holman, F. 1983. *The Wild Children*. New York: Puffin.

Newkirk, T. 1989. *Critical Thinking and Writing: Reclaiming the Essay*. Urbana, IL: National Council of Teachers of English.

Probst, R. E. 1992. "Writing from, of, and about Literature." In *Reader Response in the Classroom*, ed. Nicholas J. Karolides, 117-127. New York: Longman.

Rosenblatt, L. M. 1983. *Literature As Exploration*, 4th ed. New York: Modern Language Association.

Sebestyen, O. 1989. *The Girl in the Box*. New York: Bantam.

Voigt, C. 1982. *Homecoming*. New York: Fawcett Juniper.

————. 1986. *Izzy Willy-Nilly*. New York: Fawcett Juniper.

————. 1985. *The Runner*. New York: Scholastic.

Six

What's Age Got to Do with It? Adults Respond to Young Adult Literature

Writing [The Chocolate War] *had been an exhilirating experience for me. I wrote with all the craft I could summon. More than craft, passion. I was emotionally involved with the characters and events, though I wondered, as I wrote, who would ever read this strange novel about high school students involved in a candy sale. I did not know at that time about the young adult audience, did not know that such a market existed. All I knew was that the novel rang true to me.*

Robert Cormier

What do you read for pleasure? This is a question I often ask my college students, especially those who are working toward graduate degrees in English. Responses vary, with most people citing contemporary works by authors such as Jane Smiley, Don DeLillo, Anne Tyler, or Pat Conroy. These students, many of whom are secondary school teachers, seem surprised when I ask whether they have read, purely for their own enjoyment, any works classified as young adult literature. "Sometimes my students will recommend these books to me," one woman said, "but when I go to a bookstore to buy a book for myself, it doesn't occur to me to browse through the young adult section. I guess I just want something with a little more substance. Besides, I have no desire to relive my adolescence."

This woman's comments are indicative of the misconceptions adults often have about young adult literature—that it's nothing more than watered down plot, that its themes are of interest only to teenagers. If they read YA literature at all, their motivation is usually pedagogical or parental. I consider such attitudes a challenge in my graduate adolescent literature course, where we read a dozen or so young adult novels and numerous short stories in ten weeks. As part of the classwork, I require my students to write response papers to any two of the books we're reading and to lead class discussion on the day those books are assigned. The content of their papers is often stunning, belying the students' earlier assumptions about the literature and revealing an engagement that sometimes surprises even them.

Personal Response

One class session was particularly memorable. We had read Walter Dean Myers' *Fallen Angels*, and three students—two men and one woman—were leading the discussion. The class of fifteen graduate students had bonded well, and all were eager to hear the responses to this compelling novel about the physical and emotional experiences of Richie Perry, Peewee Gates, and other young soldiers in Vietnam. Sarah read her response first, pointing out that the novel is full of contradictions:

> It is about a war headed for peace erupting in the worst battles that had yet been seen, about friends fighting enemies and killing friends. It is a novel about tearing apart—the tale of a civil war in which one brother may destroy another; yet, it is also a story about pulling together—the tale of a strong friendship in which two joined strengthens each one. It is . . . a tale of angel warriors fighting to remain human.

For Sarah, the novel was "both heart-lifting and heart-wrenching," as the young soldiers struggle to cope with these contradictions. Ending her response, Sarah lamented the folly of war and the useless deaths of the innocent young men who fight it, and read a poem by Eve Merriam that poignantly captured her feelings.

Robert was struck by Myers' technique of tossing "explosive passages of prose at his readers." As an English teacher, Robert was tempted to analyze the book further but resisted the temptation, saying, "I must confess a certain hesitance to dissect this work by literary type or device; its wholeness is a tribute to Myers' craft." Instead, he talked about his own experience as a reader:

> Throughout the prewriting and drafting of this [response], I returned repeatedly to the dedicatory page. I remain amazed that Myers could so deftly control a narrative involving a war which must have had a devastating personal effect on him. In the manner of Hemingway, Myers delivers no overtly didactic messages; his words allow the readers to draw their own conclusions. I wonder if Myers himself was like Kenny [the protagonist's younger brother] waiting for letters which never arrived or were all too few in number. I wonder whether Richie Perry resembles "Sonny" Myers [the author's brother]. And I wonder how in the world Myers could even attempt first person, inject such varied and frequent humor, and ultimately allow his protagonist to survive the conflict which killed his own brother.

Struck by Myers' juxtaposition of death and humor in the book, Robert cited several examples, concluding that Myers employs this technique not as comic relief, but in an "attempt to maintain a sense of incoherence in his readers." Robert added, "both characters and readers seek stability, coherence. Instability, of course, aggravates us. War must be the epitome of incoherence, and to the very last page, Myers offers only the relief of knowing that Peewee and Richie have survived."

Finally, Robert confessed to playing "the famous 'find the title' game":

> Upon the first reading, I was disappointed that the only significance of the title was the funeral prayer spoken by Lieutenant Carroll at Jenkins' death for all "angel warriors that fall." I had expected some extended biblical allusion. It was only in the weeks following that first reading that I came to another conclusion. In religious lore, the fallen angels were, of course, those spirits banished from Paradise after greed and arrogance led them into war. Perhaps Walter Dean Myers is suggesting that whenever humankind succumbs to the folly of war, regardless of the cause, we become creatures far inferior to the lowest echelon of celestial beings. For this reason, books such as this one become important reading for young adults. Such sagas of the atrocities of battle must be available to those who are lured by the elders of any society to take up the sword.

Though Robert specifically targeted young adults as the audience for this book, it is apparent that he, too, found its content powerful and thought-provoking, a view that was shared by our third respondent, William. As an African American man, he was particularly sensitive to the plight of the protagonist, Richie Perry, and the other black soldiers in his company. Speculating that Myers may have been subtly addressing the relationship between blacks' enlistment and civilian opportunity, William pointed out that "for many young black men, the wartime option is often a simple one: headlines at home, or front-lines overseas." Commenting on the book's effect, he felt that *"Fallen Angels* holds meaning and impact for a variety of audiences. For people like me with limited knowledge of the Vietnam War, this book offers a geography and history lesson. While reading, I flipped to the book's map numerous times to see just where 'in country' the action was unfolding." William added:

> I liked this book. Although *Fallen Angels* is billed as adolescent literature, it is certainly enjoyable adult fare as well. At the core of [the book's] strengths is Myers' hauntingly realistic portrayal of the Vietnam War. Through his well-crafted, sharp depictions, Myers places readers squarely in the jungles of southeast Asia and brings home Vietnam in all its tragic significance. *Fallen Angels* reveals Vietnam as a place where the difference between "cootie" and "coon" becomes miniscule and the boundaries of patience, tolerance, rational thought, and fairness [come] together in a blur of confused tension. Furthermore, readers see Vietnam as a place where the shrapnel and mine laden realities of patrols can quickly dull a soldier's appetite for combat while simultaneously making his taste for life more urgent, more immediate—more acute.

William's paper was so passionate, so beautifully written, that I had difficulty deciding which excerpts to quote here. To fully communicate his response, I must include his concluding paragraph.

> In the end what struck me most about this book was the war's futility. *Fallen Angels* reminds us that, with the exception of a small percentage of gung-ho grunts who hold a death wish and/or a perverse sense of excitement, no one really wants to fight in these wars. I could not help but think of the 57,000 fallen angels who never had the chance to, like us, discuss Vietnam retrospectively or see just how big that thing called the Super Bowl (which Myers briefly mentions in the novel) actually became. I thought of the soldiers who returned stateside and, though luckier than Jenkins, Brew, and Lieutenant Carroll, could not possibly have been the same as they were prior to their Nam tours. I thought of Walter Dean Myers who lost a brother to the Vietnam War and how *Fallen Angels* was, perhaps, a catharsis for Myers that maybe allowed him to resolve some feelings, some emotions. Finally, I thought of all the fathers, mothers, sisters, and brothers who were somehow burned by Vietnam's fire. I thought of the pain, the anguish, the despair. War, I can only imagine and suppose, is like that.

As William finished reading, the class was stunned. Some eyes brimmed with tears. For what seemed like a long time, no one spoke. Finally, one of the students pulled a tape of Billy Joel's "Goodnight Saigon" from her purse and played it for us on a tape recorder that she had brought. She had even typed and made copies of the lyrics for the class, anticipating our reaction to the book. As I recall the occasion now, I'm filled once again with the emotion I felt on that May evening when my students showed me what can happen when a compelling piece of literature—regardless of its classification—touches the hearts and souls of its readers.

Passionate response in this class was not limited to historical fiction. Cynthia's reaction to Lois Duncan's *Daughters of Eve* was equally sincere and revealing. Though some have criticized this novel as stereotypical and lacking credibility, Cynthia saw it differently, commenting, "I cannot recall a book that has provoked more upheaval, questioning, and examination of my own perceptions of life than this novel." This was quite an admission from a teacher who had initially been skeptical of young adult literature and who strongly believed in a steady diet of the classics. Marveling at the book's effect on her beliefs, she continued:

> Although I believe in Ghandi and Martin Luther King and have watched too many school fights over "He said; she said" to be able to justify savage retribution, I cheered for the Daughters of Eve's actions when they shaved Peter's head. Certainly he, an obvious symbol of all insensitive men, deserved to experience in some small way the pain that he had so callously inflicted upon the women in his life. What I didn't realize was that Duncan had no intention of letting me off so easily. "So you'll buy that, eh?" she seems to say. "Well, then, what about this? And this? And this?" . . . When I began reading this novel, I was shocked by the insensitivity that Duncan gave her male characters. By the end of Chapter 1 I had met two rude brothers, one thoughtless father, and one ogre. I was angry! All men aren't like this. Why was Duncan doing this? Stereotypes weaken any text, don't they? However, it is through these characters that we see the murky side of men in the families of the novel. Duncan's hallmark seems to be this consistent focus on shadow and darkness.

Obviously agitated by Duncan's hold on her as a reader, Cynthia continues to explore the source of her exasperation, pointing out that the novel's formidable feminist, Irene Stark, calls to mind William Congreve's words: "Heaven has no rage like love to hatred turned/ Nor Hell a fury like a woman scorned." Speculating on the craft of the contemporary novelist, Cynthia wrote:

> The Greeks wrote works with themes of mythic proportions. Modern novelists don't often try anythic epic. Contemporary literature is more often the sophisticated work of the subtle stylist. Perhaps that is part of the reason that Duncan's kaleidoscopic scenes exasperate

me. All the stereotypes and problematic issues of the age-old RELA-
TIONSHIP between women and men are here: every argument must
be reexamined and every issue must be analyzed one more time.

Cynthia's metaphorical conclusion is thought-provoking, revealing a new understanding of the novel's power:

> Lois Duncan offers us diverse illustrations of life by changing our
> perception in kaleidoscopic disarray. Myriad jagged pieces of glass
> swirl to make countless changing pictures as the barrel is turned one
> way and then the other. Each motion changes the picture forever,
> and the exact same picture never appears again. Our lives are like
> those kaleidoscopes. Each experience and bit of knowledge changes
> forever our perception. She shows us that although we turn the bar-
> rel, sometimes the pieces continue to arrange themselves in patterns
> after we have stopped.

Since taking this adolescent literature class, and after reading
countless young adult novels on her own, Cynthia has become a con-
vert. Now, as a doctoral candidate in English education (and still a
high school teacher), she has become incredibly well read in the field
of young adult literature and brings it into her classroom at every
opportunity. She often muses about her earlier teaching days and her
self-righteous convictions about which literature should be taught in
the English class, marveling at the change that has taken place in her
thinking and in her teaching methods. Encouraging both oral and
written response from her students, Cynthia hopes their reading
experiences might also change their lives for the better in some small
way.

Lest it seem that all responses to the novels my class studied were
positive, I must relate the reaction that occured when we read Robert
Cormier's *After the First Death*. Corinne and David had quite disparate
views about the novel, and the contrast revealed an engagement that
belies any conviction that young adult literature is meaningful only to
teenagers. Corinne was angry. Strongly objecting to the book's subject
matter, she described it as "excessively violent" and "hauntingly
dark." Relentless in her criticism, she lashed out at Cormier:

> There is something obscene about a writer who steps on human
> emotions, sacrificing innocence, courage, and trust in the interest of
> furthering humanity's destructive, self-serving downside, just as
> there is something inconceivable in his creating monstrous adult role
> models, consumed only by causes and misplaced duties. . . . Unques-
> tioning in philosophy, emotionless in character, machine-like in pur-
> pose and direction, and murderous in action, they are the reigning
> forces to whom Cormier surrenders the positive, innocent, and cou-
> rageous influences found in Ben, Kate, and Raymond [the young

protagonists]. This multi-perspective on terrorism, death, disguises, and emotional despair left me empty and pondering not the frightening aspects of modern life, but rather Cormier's attitude in writing this book for an adolescent audience.

Throughout her response, Corinne's primary concern seemed to be the young people for whom she thought Cormier wrote the book. Concerned for their welfare, she saw no redeeming value in the novel, though she did appreciate Cormier's craft:

> While I strongly object to its subject matter, Cormier's book is, nonetheless, a skillfully written thriller. . . . [It is] a fine piece of writing possessing . . . great literary value in terms of poetic language, plot structure, interior monologue, description, rhythm and symbolism. Reading every other chapter, we are given two separate and complete stories, parallel, yet tightly and masterfully woven together, each differing in terms of point-of-view, rhythm, and mood.

In contrast, David saw *After the First Death* as a treatise of sorts, socially valuable as a "systems novel"—which David describes as a "post-postmodern work which goes beyond a discussion of the post World War II American mass society class system by discussing other systems that have emerged as a result of that earlier system." Equating it with Don DeLillo's *White Noise*, David goes beyond the novel's appeal to young adults to its significance to society in general:

> *After the First Death* . . . examines systems and the effects one can have upon the other. Most notably, Cormier places the system of post World War II nationalism (called patriotism by the Americans and dedication to a non-existent homeland by the hijackers) in opposition to the family structure. The blind allegiance of both sides to the system of nationalism (defined as a devotion to national interests, unity and independence) causes the characters to act on two levels and is the basis for the novel's action. In the novel, Delta also exists as Inner Delta and General Marchand as General Rufus Briggs because there is a need, created by nationalism, to preserve an American ethic. . . . [Yet] the family structure, usually an important part of the American ethic Inner Delta seeks to protect, is set aside to protect other nationalistic goals perceived as more important—in this case, the ability of America to protect its own interests.

In his conclusion, David speculates that Cormier's purpose in the novel is "to show that the system of nationalism, the cause of probably every major armed confrontation of our time, is powerful enough to tear down the most basic segments of American life—families and the father-son relationship."

Though differences in gender and avocation (Corinne teaches adolescents, while David teaches college students) may account for some of the contrast in these two responses, we can't discount the ability of the work itself to produce such reactions. If a text does not exist without a reader, then Corinne and David have brought *After the First Death* to life in accordance with their own expectations and experience. That the novel holds up under their scrutiny—whether their response be anger or affirmation—takes it out of the limiting realm of young adult novel and places it in the broader category of good books that can be read and enjoyed by any intelligent reader.

Also included in our reading list for this class was a work of nonfiction by Robert Sam Anson entitled *Best Intentions: The Education and Killing of Edmund Perry*, a journalist's account of the education and tragic death in June 1985 of a promising young black man in Harlem. Eddie Perry had just graduated from the prestigious Phillips Exeter Academy and had accepted a full scholarship to Stanford University, when he was found dead in the gutter late one night—shot by an undercover policeman whom Perry had apparently tried to rob. Through a series of interviews and other investigation, Anson reconstructs the events that led to Perry's demise, focusing on the young man's increasing stress as he tried to live in two different worlds while feeling secure in neither. My students found the book compelling, but the most intense response came from Chantelle, who had experienced many of the problems Eddie encountered. She began

> My mind is swarming with thoughts. I don't know if I'm angry or not about the circumstances surrounding Edmund Perry's death. I will not allow myself to fall into the trap my cultural conditioning has taught me, blame the white man for everything and to hell with the facts. That attitude is wrong. It stems from ignorance. I am not ignorant. . . . It is the mentality of a great deal of the black culture that if you speak grammatically correct, rarely use slang and never use Black English you're acting white. If black individuals enjoy music and clothing from other cultures, carry themselves in a confident manner, and never waiver about their rights to have the best life has to offer, they're acting white. . . . Well, I know who I am. I have never rejected my black roots or my black identity. I coexist very well in both the white and black cultures; and I don't have to make a conscious effort to do it.

Obviously angry about the memories the book had triggered, Chantelle asked a series of rhetorical questions about her language, her clothing, her education, and her goals, wondering why others of her race reject people like her who are trying to achieve the best in life. Connecting her experience to Eddie's, Chantelle wrote:

> I'm damn tired of being subjected to this criticism and ridicule by people of my own race. It is so sad that they cannot see by acting in

this way they discourage the black children of tomorrow from going after their dreams. The ones who do go after their dreams and achieve them are made to feel guilty for having succeeded. Eddie felt this guilt and didn't know how to handle it. It was not necessary for him to choose between embracing the white or black culture. He could have peacefully coexisted in both. He did not know this and no one ever told him. The lack of this knowledge destroyed him.

Chantelle's response reminds us of how powerful a book can be in stirring our emotions and increasing our self-understanding. The fact that Eddie Perry was a seventeen-year-old prep school student while Chantelle was an adult graduate student and single mother made no difference in the level of her engagement with the story. Anson's book reads like a mystery, and while most people in the class found it intriguing, none responded as strongly as Chantelle—because she had lived it. Her response made Eddie's story more immediate for all of us in the class, enhancing our experience with the book.

Pedagogical Response

It's not surprising that teachers often respond to young adult literature in terms of how their students might react to the work or how they might use it in their classrooms. This is exactly what happens year after year when teachers submit entries to an essay contest for teachers that we offer as part of our annual English Festival at Youngstown State University. The entrants are asked to either write an essay that deepens the reader's understanding of any book on the festival booklist, or develop a stimulating pedagogical approach to that book. The teachers overwhelmingly choose a pedagogical response.

Studying Censorship: Running Loose

In 1992, our guest author at the English Festival was Chris Crutcher, whose books have been the source of much controversy—not among the young adults who read them, but among their parents and teachers. Prompted by community objections to Crutcher's novel *Running Loose*, Jeanine, who teaches at a parochial high school in the city, designed a project in which her eleventh graders did research on some of the most frequently challenged books. Her essay, "Censuring the Censors," in which she describes the project and its results, won first prize in the contest.

After brainstorming about possible reasons for attacking a book, Jeanine's students divided into groups and "raid[ed] school, public, and university libraries in search of answers." In addition, Jeanine "invited the school librarian to class to give background information on how librarians decide censorship issues and what procedures [are followed] if a book is questioned." Since her students had read *Running Loose* in order to participate in the festival, Jeanine focused primarily on that book. She read aloud the three passages that received the most objections, and invited the students' comments. The class discussed the infamous popcorn box incident, wherein villain-of-sorts Boomer Cowans claims to have seduced the popular Adrienne Klinner at the drive-in by inserting "Ol' Norton" through a hole in the bottom of the box. They talked about the morality of protagonist Louie Banks' father lying to his wife about Louie's having spent the weekend alone with his girlfriend at her father's summer cottage. Finally, the students struggled with the morality of Louie's near sexual encounter with his girlfriend, Becky. Jeanine wrote:

> Students commented on the author's parenthetical comments, noting Boomer's father's behavior—"Boomer's dad doesn't let him cuss—beats him up when he hears it—so Boomer calls his 'thing' Ol' Norton" (Crutcher, 12)—as part of the reason for Boomer's bizarre behavior and lack of proper vocabulary for his genitals. Unexpectedly, they dismissed the "Boomer-popcorn-Norton/thing" story, instead focusing on a few lines that appear a line or two later as proof that censors should focus on more than one passage to discover what Crutcher clearly intended. "He's so dumb he doesn't know every jerk in the world has told that story. I mean, Adrienne Klinner would have poured her Coke into the box and taken a bus back to Trout" (12). They cited various other boasts that almost everyone had heard, appeared to believe, but dismissed as just that—feeble locker room attempts to impress. They cited Louie's words two pages later as a more accurate description of their feelings: "I spend about half my life worrying about hurting other people's feelings and wondering if they like me. . . . Like one of the reasons I never made it with a girl was I was afraid she'd cry and feel crappy when it was over." (14)

Jeanine ends by describing perhaps the most important insight that her students gained from this project:

> They concluded that their original easy generalizations of "We've heard worse than that on the streets," or "How can we decide for ourselves if we can't read these books?" were just that—empty generalizations. . . . They decided not to accept one group's or one person's perspective of any issue—however inflammatory. Ultimately, as one student succinctly suggested, they learned "not to censure the censors," a fitting summation to an intriguing, ever-present First Amendment dilemma that even the Supreme Court has not resolved to everyone's satisfaction.

Writing to Understand Our Lives: The Pigman

Another prize-winning essay was written the following year in response to Paul Zindel's *The Pigman*. Victoria, who teaches tenth-grade English at a suburban high school, saw a real connection between James Britton's work on writing to understand and Paul Zindel's writing motivation. "As I read all three of the Paul Zindel English festival selections," she wrote, "I noted that much of Zindel's work reflects his own desire to address unresolved, personal experiences." Victoria observed that "Zindel's understanding of [the] need to write about what concerns him or what frightens him . . . enables him to create fictional characters who also rely on the power of writing"— namely, John and Lorraine, the protagonists in *The Pigman*.

Victoria's essay goes on to describe several ways in which writing is liberating for John and Lorraine after the Pigman's death, for which they feel responsible. She summarizes:

> Both Lorraine and John have used the writing process to sort out their many feelings of guilt, grief, and blame, and ultimately, they better understand their experience with Pigman. In the last chapter of the book, students sense the degree to which the experience *and* the writing of the experience have affected John and Lorraine.

In her conclusion, Victoria underscores the importance of writing to understand and empower ourselves, admitting that this message is often lost on students.

> Convincing high school students . . . can be a challenge. Not all students are like Lorraine and John. Many consider writing as merely something they must do for their English teachers; therefore, it is rarely a reflective or an enlightening process. Teachers, however, can use Zindel's *The Pigman* as a springboard for discussing the role writing plays in their lives and for exposing students to the possibilities writing affords them. John and Lorraine are likeable characters with whom students identify, and within the context of discussing John and Lorraine's compelling desire to write this story, students discover that writing can be a powerful and liberating force.

Listening to Other Views: Nothing but the Truth

Student writing surfaced again in a prize-winning response essay written by Linda. Her school was involved in a pilot program using interactive distance learning. Because of school rivalries, Linda's creative writing students were refusing to interact with their peers from other schools. Each faction told a different story about where the fault for the rivalry lay, so Linda decided to seize a teachable moment and offer a lesson in point of view to her creative writers. While her first inclination was to use Faulkner's *As I Lay Dying* as her text, she decided on a work that she felt was equally intriguing, yet more accessible to her students—Avi's *Nothing but the Truth*. She explained:

> I found *Nothing but the Truth* by Avi an exceptional tool for helping students understand how circumstances are drastically altered, depending upon one's point of view. Moreover, it is a perfect tool for a class where the primary focus is writing, since it can be read as a "weekend assignment," and the beneficial discussion that followed the reading of this work not only enabled my creative writers to come to terms with the often elusive ability to think of themselves as "story tellers" separate from the tale they tell but also provided them with the means to discuss and eventually understand that unique evolution of "misunderstandings" which can become formidable entities indeed.

The story focuses on Philip Malloy, a high school student who insists on humming "The Star-Spangled Banner" each morning in homeroom, even though the conduct code instructs everyone to remain at "respectful silent attention." After several attempts to silence Philip, his homeroom teacher, Miss Narwin (who is also his English teacher), sends him to the principal. A series of miscommunications results in the involvement of less-than-competent administrators, an opportunistic school board candidate, and, finally, members of the press—who claim that Philip's First Amendment rights have been violated. Everyone has a different story to tell—some less informed than others—and what started as a school matter becomes a media event, with Philip and Miss Narwin caught at the center. Though she is one of the best teachers in the school, Miss Narwin is finally forced to resign, and Philip transfers to another school, leaving the reader to ponder the injustice of it all.

Of her students' experience with the book, Linda said

> My students learned one of the most important lessons any one of us can ever learn. Ironically, they didn't learn it from me but from each other. It was a lesson made possible through Philip's pain and technological advances in education.... They learned that the boundaries set for them by district lines, team rivalries, and misleading stereotypes can be erased; they learned that people everywhere have hopes, and goals, and fears, and tribulations.... And they learned that the only way to avoid the obstacles that each one of us, deliberately or inadvertently, will undoubtedly encounter is through honest and unconditional communication.

The Community Book Club

All of the preceding responses were elicited by either class work or a writing competition, but an equally interesting response occurred when a group of adults decided to form a book-study group focusing on young adult literature. Meeting once a month to discuss such works as Lois Lowry's *The Giver*, Robert Cormier's *Fade*, and Caroline Cooney's *The Cheerleader*, these ten people explained and argued their way through these books, offering varying perspectives and nudging each other toward a better understanding of the works.

Perhaps the most powerful reaction was in response to *The Giver*, a Newbery Award-winning futuristic novel about a seemingly ideal society free of conflict, injustice, and inequality in which only one person, the Giver, is the keeper of memories. The story revolves around twelve-year-old Jonas, who has been assigned by the Elders to take over the role of the Giver from the aging man who has held it for many years. Jonas becomes the Receiver of Memory through his apprenticeship to the Giver, gradually discovering the secrets behind his outwardly perfect world. What Jonas learns horrifies him, forcing him to make difficult decisions about his future role in this society.

As the study group convened, everyone was eager to talk about the book. Some noted that they had waited impatiently for the meeting date, wishing it had been earlier so they could hear others' reactions to the novel. One woman said immediately, "I loved the book. The discovery of emotions was really touching. It struck memories in me, too. The realization of color—the red in the apple and the hair—was absolutely fantastic." (In this society there was an absence of color, but every once in a while Jonas had a glimpse of something bright, the significance of which he didn't quite understand.)

"At first I thought it was utopian," said Eric, "but toward the end I really got the feeling that this isn't utopian at all because it's what parts of our society are leaning toward, sameness."

Ted chimed in, "One of the things that really worked for me is the fact that there was in the book, at least for a while, a real tension about whether this was good or bad. I as a reader, by the time I was done, realized how horrific this society was, but, you know, there are some seductively wonderful qualities that it has, and I appreciated those as I was following along in the story. That was important to me as a reader because it wasn't some sort of cliche that said, 'This is a totalitarian society and we've got to get rid of it.' It was carefully done. I think you're right. What's so neat about it is that a lot of the appeal this society has is exactly what *we* seem to value as a society—or pretend that we value, anyway."

Sandra added, "I thought there was a lot of irony with those names in a society such as this—to have these Christian names [Jonas, Gabriel, Lily] where there seemed to be life without any kind of personal religion or spirituality."

"I want a female perspective on this," said Eric, "but I was bothered by something. At first I thought, 'Oh, good, a father who's a nurturer, a mother who's a judge, and a boy who wants to be a nurturer'—but it's a false world! . . . I think this is a wonderful book for young people, but does it then take the stereotypes and say, 'See, they're good. Can't have fathers being nurturers. Can't have mothers being judges. Doesn't work'?"

"I don't think that's what it does," replied Ted, "because I don't think it draws that much attention to gender in that way. They really are asexual, and there's a sense in which, in our conventional way, that isn't an issue at all. I think the issue is—and that's why I thought it was so seductive—that they're so thoughtful and careful to know what each person's strength is, and it strikes me as a good thing that they had found a way to not let gender be an issue."

"I think the book is seductive," said Sandra, "not just that view of society because it's orderly and everything's carefully done, but when you recognize that—when Jonas is seeing color for the first time— that central character was so interesting to me. I just was absorbed with the character, and I haven't had a chance to go back and see exactly how the author accomplished it, but I found that character really intriguing and true to what children are like."

Sheila, a child psychologist, agreed. "I love the description of how Jonas is slowly set apart, and how that's so accurate for the way the story begins. All of a sudden he's just not quite fitting in, and then there's this slow feeling of being different from people."

That the word *seductive* appears quite often in this dialogue is interesting. While it may have been a case of the participants seizing on a word that sounded good and repeating it almost unconsciously, it also indicates a real engagement with the novel—a conclusion that's strengthened by the comments about the character of Jonas and the society that Lowry has created in the book. These adults' reactions to the novel reveal a concern for the kind of universal issues and problems that transcend literary categorization. They could just as easily have been talking about the dystopian societies of Huxley's *Brave New World* or Orwell's *1984*.

Though the reaction to Lowry's novel was overwhelmingly positive, the group's response to Robert Cormier's *Fade* was not. Many felt that it was not a book for young adults, and some criticized the author for writing what they considered to be a potboiler. To clarify matters, one of the group members, who had read an interview with the author, explained that Cormier thought of *Fade* as his *"adult* adult book." It is, however, read mainly by young adults and appears with Cormier's other novels in the young adult section in bookstores and libraries. Primarily about the life of writer Paul Moreau, who has inherited the family curse of invisibility, the novel contains scenes of incest and pedophilia, as well as violence that is sometimes perceived as gratuitous. As with Cormier's other novels, the book uses a disjointed plot structure. The story begins in Moreau's adolescence, and as it continues, introduces other characters who connect with Moreau in various ways at times. Like all of Cormier's works, the book is disturbing, a reaction echoed by all in the group.

"I couldn't sleep after I read this," remarked one woman. "It still bothers me," said another. "There were times when I didn't know what to think." After some discussion of Cormier's tendency to set evil deeds in religious institutions, as he does in both *The Chocolate War* and *Fade*, Eric jumped into the conversation "Well, I'm probably going to get kicked out of this club for saying this, but this guy is an irascible curmudgeon. I've said that before, and I say it again. This guy has at least three or four loose screws. He writes this beautiful book—this is wonderful—all these rhetorical things going on—he changes point of view, he does this, he does that, and then he says 'I had Stephen King endorse this, so on the last page I want you to know there's going to be a sequel.' We're ba-a-a-ck! It's cheap! So when you talk about it being an adult book, and he's got his heart and soul in it—he's a writer! He wants to make money."

"You're really making me mad!" replied Barbara. "I love this man!"

"Yeah, I know," said Eric, "but this is my last line. Listen to this—my horse race line. [Reads from comments he had written down.] This entry was strong out of the gate, record-setting times at the splits, and then in the stretch it did fade."

"Could your attitude toward him have anything to do with the way you read the book?" asked Gina.

"I loved it!" Eric replied. "I said, 'Wow, this is really suspenseful; this is a fun read.' I enjoyed it. I had trouble putting it down—until the last two pages."

"Well, I didn't like it long before the last two pages," interjected Nancy. "I tried this book about two years ago, and I thought it was slow, plodding, and I just couldn't really get into it. *After the First Death* is one of my favorite books of all time. I could read that book and read that book, and *I Am the Cheese* is the same way. There's a circularity to it that I expect from him. I don't expect a book that's linear, and at the end of this I said, 'So What?' I felt that Cormier played games with this book that I didn't feel with the others. I felt like Ozzie [Paul

Moreau's nephew, who also inherits the family curse and commits some violent acts because of it] was a device, and I guess I would have been happier if Paul had just told his own story and maybe given me a hint. That would have been much more 'Robert Cormier.' I was very disappointed in this book. I just didn't find the depth in the plot. In the characters there's always good stuff, but in the plot—that's what I look for in Cormier—a resonance in the plot of the complexity of the characters because he has such complex characters. And the plots are so complex that they bring you back into the characters and give you something to really chew on, and I didn't find that in here. I think the book faded."

"I think that's why he's playing with point of view, though," Eric replied. "It's mostly narration—consider all the narrators—so he's experimenting, and then the 'Ozzie' section is third-person point of view. So he's constantly making it incoherent for us as readers. I like that because it makes good suspense. I think it's an experiment, and that's where you have to decide if the experiment works or if it fails."

Sarah argued, "But that just refutes everything you just said about its being written just for money."

"Oh! But it's an experiment!" Eric reminded her. "Because he says, 'Now I've written something really obtuse here, and does this stay in my room, or do people actually buy this?' Well, guess what? It's in paperback—people are buying it! He loves it!"

"But why would he have to resort to a cheap trick when he's already a best-selling author and he's already made tons and tons of money?" asked Gina.

"Good question!" Eric said. "Why does he make the girl die in *After the First Death*? I mean, he has some very strange views of life. Very strange. I don't need everything to be rose-colored, but I want things every once in a while to be . . . redemptive, maybe? You know, Ozzie had to die. Okay. Ozzie *had* to die. I buy that. Very tender, well-written scene. But why does somebody else have to come back at the end? 'There's another one out there—so don't close your drapes!' Come on! He resorted to a cheap trick because this is an experiment."

Eric's criticism of *Fade* was sincere, as was Nancy's, and they challenged Cormier as any intelligent reader would challenge any author whose work was disappointing. While Nancy's criticism was formalistic—attacking mainly what she perceived as a weakness in plot—Eric's was more broadly based, questioning the author's motivation and its effect on the book's quality. Lost somewhere in the heated discussion was the earlier concern that the book was not suited to young adults. Any lines of categorization that had been drawn quickly disappeared when talk turned to the book as a work of art. These readers encountered a text that moved them to anger, disappointment, and confusion, and they did what most readers in that situation would do—they attacked the author.

Fade was not the only book that moved this group to harsh criticism. Having heard so much about the current explosion in young adult horror fiction, they decided to read something representative of that genre. They settled on Caroline Cooney's *The Cheerleader*. Not all of Cooney's fiction is of the horror variety, so the group felt that her work might be a step above "horror for horror's sake." The book's protagonist, Althea, wants more than anything to be a popular cheerleader, so she makes a Faustian pact with a vampire who lives in the tower of her Gothic-style home to get what she wants. In order to achieve popularity, however, Althea must "give" some of her friends to the vampire, who virtually sucks the life out of them and leaves them as shells of their former selves. In the end, Althea sees the error of her ways and manages to defeat the vampire. She walks away from him and from her ill-gotten popularity, determined to achieve popularity on her own.

As the group sat down to discuss the book, Ted pulled a folded paper from his pocket and smoothed it out on the table in front of him. After a few people made unkind jokes about the plot of the book, Ted got serious. "I sat down at the computer last night and pounded this out," he said, "and I have to read it to you." His writing turned out to be a dialogue with himself about the book:

> I have just finished reading *The Cheerleader*, and I'm so damn mad that no vampire, or human for that matter, would dare to take me on. This little young adult thriller novel is so weak and so offensive and so shallow and so demeaning that the reader . . . is left with nothing but rage at its stupidity, enough rage to throw the damn book into a tower, shutter it in, and feel the bright sunlight of decency once again. I've never condoned censorship, but I've almost never been so tempted.
>
> —C'mon, Ted. Jeez, you're overreacting. Maybe this isn't a classic, but lighten up. After all, at least Cooney knows how to tell a good story.
>
> —The hell she does. The plot is unspeakably thin here. Despite the fact that I didn't know how Althea was going to defeat the vampire, after the first twenty pages, *I didn't care*. There was never any suspense built. Plot structure consisted of "Vampire tempts girl with popularity, girl agrees and gets popularity, vampire gets victim, girl feels remorse, but girl still *really* wants to be popular. So vampire tempts girl again, and girl gets sucked in again, and. . . ." Be still, my heart. I'm almost faint with the suspense.
>
> —Well, OK, but the writing's not bad. Cooney does capture the villainy of the vampire, and the bubble-headed behaviors of the cheerleaders. She can create a character.

—Are you kidding? I don't care about any of these characters, not one. They're all stereotypes. . . . And her descriptions! She's the queen of the terrible, horrible, no-good metaphor. "His skin was a spongy mushroom." "Pain like bread knives with serrated edges sawed through Althea's heart." Gad, I'm going to retch!
—But the lesson of this morality play? How about the good point it makes that young people shouldn't sell their souls to a vampire, or to anyone, to gain popularity? Don't kids need such a lesson? And isn't this an entertaining way to deliver it?
—Now you've come to the point. . . . My God, this isn't a cautionary tale about the dangers of popularity. Instead, it actually affirms the creed that adolescence *is* all about popularity, after all. The message of this book is that the cult of popularity lives, and that young girls especially need to thirst after it. . . . I can't stand what this story did to women. The bubble-headed cheerleader . . . is revered here. And the cult of popularity puts these girls in the worst kind of self-imposed captivity. . . . This book really gutted me out. . . . Even as a supposedly momentary pleasure, even as a bit of linguistic mastur-bation, the bottom line is I just can't let *The Cheerleader* be. This book isn't just weak, and it isn't just bad. It is . . . (yes, I use the word defiantly) evil. *The Cheerleader* is an evil book.

Whew! The group was speechless. Ted had summed up the general reaction to the book, but the depth and passion of his response gave everyone something to think about. Teenage horror fiction has been roundly criticized by many teachers who fear its effect on the young in an alarmingly violent society, but Ted's response addresses the equally dangerous issue of misguided goals achieved at the cost of human ethics and compassion. To those who say that young adult literature has nothing to offer anyone over eighteen, Ted's reaction is a reminder that even the weakest work can evoke strong emotion in an adult and may, if shared by a skillful teacher with young adult readers, result in students reading such a book from a more critical perspective as they look beyond the literal meaning. Horror fiction is not about to go away, and teenage horror fiction is big business for publishers. Somebody's buying and reading these books, and it isn't adults—all the more reason for awareness on the part of teachers and parents.

Perhaps my student who said that she wanted to read something with a little more substance than young adult literature just hadn't read enough in the genre. Surely the responses of the adults noted here refute the claim that young adult literature is of interest only to teenagers. As Eric noted during a discussion of Virginia Euwer Wolff's beautifully poetic novel *Make Lemonade*, "These books aren't for children. They aren't for adolescents. These are everybody's books. To say that *Make Lemonade* should be pointed to a specific age group is sad."

Adults who aren't teachers or parents miss a great deal by walking past the shelves labeled young adult literature in libraries and bookstores. Until responses like those noted here begin to dispel the myth that YA literature is lightweight, until adult readers can convince the reading public that these are everybody's books, we'll continue to be secret sharers of literature that not only encourages us to remember, but also reminds us how important it is not to forget.

Works Cited

Anson. R. S. 1987. *Best Intentions: The Education and Killing of Edmund Perry.* New York: Vintage.

Avi. 1991. *Nothing but the Truth.* New York: Avon.

Cooney, C. B. 1991. *The Cheerleader.* New York: Scholastic.

Cormier, R. 1979. *After the First Death.* New York: Dell.

———. 1988. *Fade.* New York: Dell.

Crutcher, C. 1983. *Running Loose.* New York: Dell.

Duncan, L. 1979. *Daughters of Eve.* New York: Dell.

Lowry, L. 1993. *The Giver.* New York: Dell.

Myers, W. D. 1988. *Fallen Angels.* New York: Scholastic.

Wolff, V. E. 1993. *Make Lemonade.* New York: Scholastic.

Zindel, P. 1978. *The Pigman.* New York: Bantam.

Seven

Responding to Response

Every reader's response matters. Writers need readers to complete the work of the book. That's not something we're often taught in school.

Sandy Asher

As both a teacher and an interested reader, I can't resist making a few observations about what is documented in the chapters of this book and what I've seen in my research of the last two years. As I've watched and listened to readers interact with young adult novels in various circumstances, I've become more convinced than ever of the folly of labeling literature according to who should read it. Just a glance at what took place with the advanced placement students described in Chapter 3 and the adult readers in Chapter 6 is enough to trigger regret that certain literature has limited exposure because it happens to focus on the lives of people between the ages of twelve and eighteen. I hope you'll compare the observations of mine that follow with your own and that my thoughts might initiate a dialogue about YA literature that will continue into the future.

Young Adult Literature Across Learning Tracks

Engagement was the order of the day for most students, regardless of their academic ability, when they read Robert Cormier's *After the First*

Death. Because they cared about and could identify with the characters, students entered the world of the book almost automatically—slipping into the bus seat next to Kate, sitting with Miro and Artkin in the restaurant, standing next to Ben on the bridge. No matter what their reading level, the students wondered about Artkin's use of "the fingers" to torture Ben; wanted to understand why General Marchand sacrificed his son Ben for "the cause"; and condemned Miro for killing Kate. And, interestingly enough, all the students focused on Miro more than any other character in their writing and discussion. Something about him put them in touch with their own loss of innocence, with a contradiction in themselves unconsciously suppressed.

Basic Ninth Graders

Perhaps the most surprising reaction came from the ninth graders in the basic class, who weren't expected to understand the novel—or even read it by themselves. Though there were probably several who lived up (or down) to this expectation, the students who did read and discuss the book showed remarkable insight for supposed nonreaders. The males in the class were most vocal—perhaps because of the book's subject matter—but one or two female students showed an active interest in Kate. I found it intriguing that those who took part in the discussion—Jason and Derek—were confident of their interpretations and seemed unaware that they were tackling the most difficult aspects of the book. I wonder what might have happened if their teacher hadn't led the book discussion with questions— whether the students would have talked more about their own reactions to the book, as they began to do in the collaborative activity "Hit Vids!"

As a result of my research I became particularly interested in Jason, who, as I noted in Chapter 1, contradicted all my assumptions about reluctant readers. Through more investigation I learned that Jason was mostly a D student, and had received one B in a reading class in junior high. Raised by his grandparents, he fell into bad company early and had missed over forty days of school the previous year. While the missionary in me wanted to take Jason by the hand and lead him down the path of literacy, the realist in me said that the Jasons of the world are on their own—unless the system changes. And we teachers are, after all, part of the system. Somehow we have to find ways to plug the cracks that the Jasons keep falling through. We may be holding one of those plugs in our hands when we hold a young adult novel. YA literature isn't the answer to everything, but we have to start somewhere.

Advanced Ninth Graders

Just as I was pleased to see the confidence with which the basic ninth graders expressed their views in discussions, I was a little surprised at the tentativeness of the advanced students when they discussed *After the First Death* among themselves in small groups. They were just as curious about the novel's events as the other students were, but they felt more secure asking their teacher for the answers to difficult questions than they did developing those answers themselves. I attribute this to the students' conditioning and to their emphasis on getting the "right" answer, and I see a potential problem in the students' lack of confidence in their own interpretation skills. It's not my intention here to disparage the literary classics, but we can't ignore the way these more difficult pieces of literature may influence student confidence. If readers in advanced classes are accustomed to waiting to hear their teacher's interpretation of a work before they venture one of their own, they may think twice—especially if a grade is involved—before they make a definite statement about any work. In Chapter 2, for example, we saw the students who felt it necessary to ask Marcia whether or not Artkin was Miro's "first death." When, instead of giving a straight answer, Marcia tried to lead the students to come to their own conclusion, the group remained unsure. This is only one documented incident, of course, but in classroom observations over the years I've seen many similar occurrences. It seems to me that this is a matter worthy of more study.

Advanced Placement Twelfth Graders

Unlike the advanced ninth graders, the advanced placement seniors had no lack of confidence in expressing their interpretations. Perhaps this tells us that such insecurities go away as students mature, or perhaps it means that academically insecure ninth graders don't go on to advanced placement work. Whatever it means, the students I observed subjected the young adult literature they read to the same kind of scrutiny they gave other literary works. These particular students were in their second year of AP English, so they were well trained in the art of discussion. There *was* a difference in the level of intensity between the two classes I observed, just as there was a difference in the aspects of the novel they chose to discuss. The AP students were certainly more global in their concerns than were the ninth graders, and their discussions focused on the more sophisticated concepts of tragedy and existentialism.

As I sat in on classes with these students and read their writing, I sensed a real tension between what they thought was good reading and what they felt was good for them. As the transcripts in Chapter 3 reveal, their talk was directed by teachers' questions about the nature of tragedy in *After the First Death* and the existential philosophy in *Running Loose*, though we do get some idea of their personal identification with the works—especially with *Running Loose*. The tension is more apparent, though, in the students' written answers to my questions about reading young adult literature in the AP class. Their comments give me the feeling that, on the one hand, they have an image to uphold—the image of the super smart kids who read and analyze only the most difficult literature; but, on the other hand, they want to understand the power of literature—the power felt when a book connects to their lives, moving them to anger, frustration, or tears. For these students, the difference seems to be between intellectual engagement and emotional engagement. While they were intellectually intrigued by Meursault's actions in *The Stranger*, for example, they were emotionally challenged by Louie Banks' moral courage in *Running Loose*. Such polarities created a conflict for them: How can an American novel about a seventeen-year-old protagonist, written only a few years ago by a relatively new author, compare with a French classic, written in 1942 by a man who later won the Nobel Prize for Literature? Though such a question smacks of literary snobbery, conflicts like this are of real concern to students trying to feel their way across the political landscape of academe.

The answer is that there's no answer. Different literature does different things for different readers. If students come into an AP English class assuming that they're going to read only the literary classics that will help them score well on the national AP exam, the mindset is already there—and the AP exam being what it is, that mindset is justified. (In fairness to the AP test makers, they do now say that students may use appropriate young adult literature to answer open-ended exam questions; however, most of the students I observed seemed unwilling to take the risk. It's going to take much more evidence from the College Board and from AP teachers that intellectual and emotional engagement are valued equally before students feel comfortable writing about contemporary works of young adult fiction.) For the most part, high school students—especially those in AP classes—think in terms of what reading literature does *for* them, not what it does *to* them, so their ambivalence about YA literature is not surprising. As they've made their way through school, students have learned that many literature scholars disdain works enjoyed by the general public, preferring esoteric works that are inaccessible to any but the "best" minds. The credo of these scholars might be, "If you can't understand it, it must be good literature." Unless attitudes change drastically—and I don't expect they will anytime soon—young adult literature will remain, at best, a welcome diversion that helps AP students better understand the classics, but that doesn't stand on its own as a component of the AP English curriculum. What YA literature does to these students as young adult readers is another matter entirely.

Collaboration Through Young Adult Literature

When I first had the idea of bringing basic and advanced ninth graders together to work on a literature simulation in response to a young adult novel, I had misgivings. I worried that the students wouldn't talk to each other, wouldn't feel comfortable together. I fretted about the difficulty of the project—was I asking too much of them in a forty-five-minute class period? Most of all, I was concerned that the project would fail—that I would learn nothing of interest. As it turned out, I learned a great deal about how ninth graders read young adult literature, how they respond to the literature within certain constraints, and how they interact with each other in a collaborative situation.

More than ever, I'm convinced of the value of teachers and students reading and studying literature together. We have not employed collaborative study much in literature classes—even though we may see its value in teaching writing—and collaborative literature study across learning tracks is virtually unheard of. For the most part, students in literature classes read alone, answer study questions alone, and take tests alone. True, they do have the opportunity to participate in class discussion, but they are still alone with their thoughts about their reading and still alone when they venture an interpretation or a question about a work. The students who participated in the "Hit Vids!" simulation didn't have to worry about isolation. They could toss ideas at each other, reject some, accept others, and come up with a variety of responses to *After the First Death*. I'm sure the experience of planning and writing together resulted in learning that can't be observed or measured, learning that may surface at other times in the students' lives. Allowing students to collaborate on literature study— whether it's working through a simulation, generating questions about their reading, or answering questions they have about a work— removes the tension that often exists when students worry about having the right interpretation of a work. It offers fresh perspectives, nudging readers toward different ways of looking at a text. It encourages them to be student critics and to explore the aspects of a work that are meaningful to them, not just to perform superficial exercises designed by their teacher or a textbook. Students will become much more familiar with a work through this kind of study than they ever will by answering preconceived study questions.

My college students, many of whom are education majors, often ask me how they can study for a literature exam—particularly when they will have to answer essay questions. They are used to reading for the facts, listening to lectures, taking notes, and answering objective test questions. I tell them to study together—to talk through the literature, to review each work we've read, to ask each other questions about what puzzles them. Many of these students have commented that they learned much through this kind of study, and they invariably do well on essay questions. What I haven't yet done is give my students the opportunity to collaborate with one or two others on an exam—to write together about the works we've read, perhaps learning as they write. When I was a student this would have been called cheating. Answers were your own and not to be shared with others. You covered your paper as you wrote and turned it facedown when you were finished. The contest was to determine who was the smartest and who could remember the most. Learning didn't seem to have much to do with it. Of course, this attitude still exists in some classrooms, but more and more educators are becoming aware that true learning is an *experience*, not an exercise. The only cheating occurs when students are denied the chance to have such an experience.

Allowing students to study literature collaboratively has benefits for teachers, too. Our first thought might be, "Yes! A lighter paper load!" but there are even better reasons to encourage working together. We teachers do an incredible amount of preparation when we introduce a literary work. In addition to reading the work again and again to refresh our memories, we generate questions for students to answer, create activities and projects related to the literature, compose lecture material, and devise test questions. Then we must orchestrate discussions, field questions, and generally try to keep students interested in the literature. And we do this for each work we teach. No wonder we're exhausted. We're doing all the work. Why not spread it around a little? If we know our John Dewey, we should remember that students learn by doing (or as one of my cornier professors put it, "learn by Dewey-ing"), and this applies to literature study, too. Self-preservation aside, we must get our students involved in the reading and study of literature if we ever hope to make the works come alive for them.

Young adult literature is the perfect vehicle for encouraging this kind of involvement, since the works are so accessible to students. It might even be worthwhile to let students try their hand at teaching a short story or two to the class, in pairs or in small groups. I guarantee that they will know the work thoroughly by the time they finish.

(Such an exercise can help you learn what kind of teacher you have been, since students will usually model their teaching after yours.) I'm not advocating that we let students do our jobs, but that we give them a chance to really come to know the literature through teaching it. It's often beneficial for students to evaluate themselves after teaching a lesson, and self-evaluation might be followed by a class discussion of the student teacher's perceived strengths and weaknesses. The more we can foster student awareness of what learning is and what's happening in the classroom, the more students will be inclined to take part in their own learning. Collaborative literature study is the perfect way for this learning to take place.

An added benefit to teachers is the opportunity to observe students in different classroom situations. Usually we see them working alone, and we evaluate their individual efforts. Having students work together gives us a chance to step back from the activity and watch the interaction, taking note of group dynamics and the individual roles that students play. My observation of Jason, for example, described in Chapter 1, revealed a student who contradicted my assumptions about so-called reluctant learners. Sometimes we pigeon-hole students, labeling them as one thing or the other, never thinking that they may be reacting to a specific classroom situation. The quiet female student in the corner, for instance, may feel uncomfortable speaking up because she's been criticized by one of the other students in the class. When she becomes part of a small group that doesn't include her critic, however, the student may reveal herself as a thoughtful conversationalist. Collaborative student activity in the classroom affords teachers the opportunity to know their students better, both personally and academically—which may translate into a more meaningful student-teacher relationship.

Making Meaning Through Written Response

A student once told me that she found it easier to write about books than to talk about them. She didn't feel confident in her ability to choose the right words to describe her response in a class discussion. Most of the time she sat and listened to others, nodding when she agreed and frowning when she didn't. Writing, she found, helped her think through her response, sometimes leading her to discover feelings about a book that she hadn't realized she had. She gave the example of Becky Sanders, Louie Banks' girlfriend in *Running Loose*. While reading the book, this student admired Becky for being a confident young woman who knew what she wanted, and she liked the fact that the author gave Becky, rather than Louie, the leading role in the relationship. As she wrote about the novel, however, the student began to feel that Chris Crutcher, the author, really hadn't portrayed Becky as a strong female at all. She decided that Crutcher had just used Becky, killing her off so she could serve her purpose in the novel. The message the student read was "Women who are stronger than men have to die." Whether or not her interpretation is plausible to other readers, there's no doubt that writing about Becky as her favorite character led this student to her conclusion—a view that she continues to hold today.

What is it about writing that clarifies thinking for us? Studies have been done to answer this question; without citing such studies, it's safe to say that capturing thoughts on a page, making them real, somehow helps us turn them around and examine them from different angles. Take the essay about "loners" in Chapter 5, for example. The student author used Bullet from *The Runner* and Anne from *Captives of Time* as her subjects. Though she starts out discussing the characters and their isolation, it becomes apparent toward the end of the essay that she really wants to talk about herself and to defend the loners of the world, among whom she counts herself. Thinking and writing about Bullet and Anne has given her insight into her own feelings about *aloneness*, which she sees as quite different from *loneliness*. As she defends Bullet and Anne, the student defends herself, and her writing might be cathartic in that respect.

A similar experience occurs for the student who wrote about two characters who donate items that are meaningful to them to a charity auction. Using characters' voices to explain why they chose the items they donated—Jackie McGee a typewriter and Izzy Lingard a mirror—this writer puts into words her reaction to these two young women, possibly understanding for the first time exactly how she feels about them. Jackie donates her precious typewriter both so that she can move on with her life and so that another person might have it as a companion. Izzy gives up her mirror so that someone else might realize that "no mirror can tell them what they look like on the inside." These are young women to admire, as this writer obviously discovers. Her final statement, in the voice of the young woman in charge of the auction, is telling: "It was then that it dawned on me that this auction wasn't just an event—it was part of people's lives, their history, and their future."

Writing about young adult literature is a natural extension of reading it. Some readers find this kind of writing a pleasant experience, while others balk at it as intrusive to their reading. But even those who resist sometimes surprise themselves with what they say. I've seen this happen in my classes, where some of the most recalcitrant writers have produced some of the most thought-provoking responses. As good as it can sometimes be, class discussion about literature does have limitations. First, students can hide if they feel they have nothing to say or if they just don't feel like talking. There are always those few who are more than happy to dominate the conversation. Sometimes the discussion is no more than a dialogue between the teacher and one or two students. Second, most discussions are teacher-directed, so they cover only what the teacher feels is important about a work. Even (maybe especially) in the advanced placement classes I observed, the students followed the teacher's lead in choosing which aspects of a book to focus on. Third, students don't have much time to think through their responses—especially when the questions come from the teacher. They seldom make the kind of discoveries that come out of written response. Though discussion is certainly useful—even necessary—as part of literature study, response should not stop there. Combining discussion with writing gives readers a chance to explore their reactions to a work, helping them make sense of their reading.

Adults Reading Young Adults

One of the things I was most curious about when I began my research was what I might find when I looked systematically at the responses of adults to young adult literature. Aside from critical and pedagogical articles by teachers and scholars, little documentation of adult response is available outside of anecdotal evidence. Why is adult response important? Because one of the loudest criticisms of young adult literature is that its appeal is limited, and adult response can either support or refute that contention. It's no secret that many adults, even teachers, are condescending in their views of young adult literature. I suspect that their attitude stems in part from the literature they remember reading as adolescents—the series books, the formulaic romances, and the career books that were common in the 1940s and 1950s. Such condescension reveals a failure to keep abreast of the latest developments in literature, which is not a good excuse for criticizing what young people are reading today.

Another less understandable and far more dangerous reason that some adults shun young adult literature is the elitist belief that anything adolescents read and enjoy must somehow be inferior in quality to adult literature. While this reasoning is likely to be more prevalent in college English departments, it exists among the general public as well. The danger of this kind of thinking is the way it stigmatizes adolescents as being a sort of less-intelligent subspecies that's incapable of literary discrimination. Because adults who hold such a belief have never read the works of authors like Robert Cormier, Cynthia Voigt, Bruce Brooks, and Kathryn Lasky, they make unwarranted assumptions based on their own uninformed biases. There is a third group also—though their number is happily decreasing. These are the adults who have never heard the term "young adult literature," even though they may have read books marketed in this category. These adults are perhaps the easiest to convince, since they come to the literature free of preconceived notions about its value.

The responses of the adults noted in Chapter 6 reveal an astonishing engagement with various works of young adult literature. Subjecting the novels to the scrutiny with which they read all literature, these adults found in the books universal elements that are sometimes missed by younger readers—evidence of the layering that characterizes all literature of quality. They approached each novel expecting the author to be skillful, thought-provoking, and entertaining. When their expectations weren't met, they attacked the aspects of the work that failed to measure up. But unlike the high school students and undergraduates who failed to see that disliking a book is often a reflection of the author's craft, these readers were quick to acknowledge the artistic skill of writers like Cormier and Myers while at the same time criticizing the writers' motivation and purpose. The charge of some critics that there is nothing to say about young adult literature is refuted in responses that identify *After the First Death* as a postmodernistic "systems novel" written in the manner of Don DeLillo's *White Noise,* and that compare the "angel warriors" in Myers' *Fallen Angels* to the fallen angels in Milton's *Paradise Lost.* Similarly, if a nonfiction work like Anson's *Best Intentions* can engender such a powerful response in a young mother of African American descent, it merits reading by other adults, for we are all responsible for a society that creates and destroys the Eddie Perrys of the world.

Not all of the adults' responses were positive. That's to be expected. But their engagement and insightful analysis should be enough to make skeptics take another look at this genre, which is producing some fine writing. Like literature classified as "adult," young adult literature does have its clunkers, but only the unfair and uninformed will judge all young adult works by the worst among them.

Responding Teachers Teaching Response

The teacher essays discussed in Chapter 6 provide some wonderful ideas for bringing response to young adult literature into the secondary school classroom. The projects described in these papers give students authority over their reading and go beyond the traditional lecture/

discussion/test approach to teaching literature. Using Chris Crutcher's work to help students learn about censorship, for example, can result in surprising insights. Unlike many adults who want to ban *Running Loose* because of what they interpret as Crutcher's endorsement of sexual experimentation, Jeanine's students were quick to see what adults frequently overlook: that Louie Banks has never "made it with a girl" because he worries about the emotional hurt he may cause. They see the "sex talk" for the macho bravado it is and recognize that it's attributed to a character who has already been discredited in the novel. Most significantly, they come to realize that the argument frequently used by young people—"We've heard worse than that on the streets"— is faulty and ineffective. As the result of their research on censorship, the students' responses to *Running Loose* become more informed and informative.

Using young adult literature to increase student awareness of how writing leads to understanding, as Victoria did with Paul Zindel's *The Pigman*, can result in a new way of thinking about writing. Victoria pinpoints a common problem with high school students: they think that writing is something to be done to please their English teachers. But after learning something about Zindel's life, then reading his novel, students see how writing fiction has become Zindel's way of working through his childhood problems. He is responding to his life, just as they respond to theirs in everything they do. If just one student discovers writing as a liberating activity as a result, reading this YA novel has been a significant literary experience.

Communication takes many forms, writing being only one, and point of view is an important factor. Students who have the opportunity to read Avi's *Nothing but the Truth* to study point of view will discover just how devastating miscommunication can be. Linda's students, who read the book to work out problems with interactive distance learning, responded by resolving their conflicts and eliminating the barriers they had constructed between themselves and students from rival schools. This kind of realization goes far beyond what traditional literature study can accomplish.

We tend to think of response to literature in terms of an oral reply or a written product, but, as demonstrated here, response can also take the form of action and reaction. The kinds of learning experiences described above won't soon be forgotten by students, and they may lead to other learning experiences later on. Young adult literature and reader response are such a natural pair that it's a mystery why more teachers haven't discovered their compatibility. There's little likelihood that students will fall asleep in class when they're reading and reacting to literature that reflects the lives they're living. And yet, teachers like Jeanine, Victoria, and Linda are still in the minority, trying hard to bring the literature curriculum to life. Far more English teachers are still trying to train their students to be literary scholars—dissecting texts, identifying similes and metaphors, looking for symbolism in every corner until the literary work is dead on arrival. We must make sure that young adult literature doesn't meet this fate, for if it does, our students will be deprived of the satisfaction that comes from first responding to a work on their own terms. In "Creating a Bond Between Writer and Reader," author Sue Ellen Bridgers gives us something to think about when she says

> I expect more quality young adult books will be written if they continue to be taught in the classrooms, suggested for book reports, and made available in the libraries and class sets—in other words, if there continues to be a market. I don't think there'll be *Cliff's Notes* for them, though, and that's a blessing in itself. (70)

Works Cited

Anson, R. S. 1987. *Best Intentions: The Education and Killing of Edmund Perry.* New York: Vintage.

Avi. 1991. *Nothing but the Truth.* New York: Avon.

Bridgers, S. E. 1992. "Creating a Bond Between Writer and Reader." In *Reading Their World: The Young Adult Novel in the Classroom*, eds. V. R. Monseau and G. M. Salvner, 65–70. Portsmouth, NH: Boynton/Cook-Heinemann.

Cormier, R. 1979. *After the First Death.* New York: Dell.

———. 1988. *Fade.* New York: Dell.

Crutcher, C. 1983. *Running Loose.* New York: Dell.

DeLillo, D. 1986. *White Noise.* New York: Penguin.

Myers, W. D. 1988. *Fallen Angels.* New York: Scholastic.

Zindel, P. 1978. *The Pigman.* New York: Bantam.

Afterword

One thing that haunts me as I reflect on what I've written here is what educators like Dora V. Smith have been saying for over sixty years: students need to participate actively in their education—to read, write about, and talk about subjects of interest to them before they can really learn. Those who know the history of education in this country know that over the years the pendulum has continually swung between the precepts of progressive and traditional education, carrying students along in its dizzying motion.

Fifty years ago Dora V. Smith taught the first adolescent literature course at the University of Minnesota, and she wrote and spoke extensively about the importance of such literature to the high school curriculum. Did people listen to her then? Not in large numbers. But some of her students—Bob Carlsen, Dwight Burton, and Walter Loban, to name a few—and their students—Ken Donelson, Stephen Dunning, Jim Davis, and others—have made a difference. Like missionaries, they've carried Smith's gospel out into the world of English education and spawned more students who continue to spread the word. But the educational system as a whole learns slowly, and traditionalism has always had a strong grip on educational practice.

As the education pendulum continues its swing, armies of students work their way through our schools, tolerating the boredom and rejoicing at the occasional class that stimulates their intellect and activates their creative energies. In spite of Dora V. Smith and the countless others who have spent entire careers trying to convince the education establishment of the value of student-centered teaching and learning, most students continue to sit in rows in quiet classrooms, reading textbooks and doing "seat work" to earn the grades that will free them to go out into the world and begin the real business of living.

But the picture is not entirely bleak. In *Schools That Work*, George Wood tells us of a few schools that are doing it right—engaging students in the kind of active learning that will last a lifetime. From the foothills of the Appalachian Mountains in rural southeastern Ohio, to New York City's Harlem, to picture-perfect New Hampshire, to the affluent suburb of Winnetka, Illinois, Wood takes us on a journey through some exemplary programs that resurrect hope for America's schools. Such programs require dedicated teachers and committed

administrators who are willing to abandon the school-as-factory metaphor in favor of a cooperative learning model. Reading groups,
worksheets, and grammar exercises are nonexistent in these programs. Curriculum is organized around themes drawn from student
interests. A set of "essential questions" guides inquiry in each area of
study. Undergirding all of this is the whole language philosophy of
teaching—a philosophy espoused long ago by Dora Smith and others
as democratic education.

A response approach to young adult literature would fit perfectly
in such programs, allowing students to read, discuss, and write about
works that add meaning to their lives. Ideally the reading would be
multicultural and cross-curricular, helping to answer the essential
questions posed for each unit of study. In her forthcoming book *Young
Adult Literature: The Heart of the Middle School Curriculum*, Lois T. Stover
advocates such an approach for middle school students, but innovative high school teachers might design a similar curriculum for their
students. Surely the responses of students and teachers described in
this book are reason enough to try.

So why aren't all of these exciting ideas making their way into the
majority of America's schools? Probably for several reasons:

- They require an entirely new, student-centered philosophy of
  teaching.
- They require cooperation among teachers and administrators.
- They require a great deal of planning on the part of teachers.
- They require approval by school boards that are composed
  largely of noneducators who know little or nothing about
  how students learn.
- They require more content knowledge on the part of teachers
  who are used to relying on textbooks.
- They require faith in students.

Given this litany of requirements, it isn't surprising that school
curricula remain largely static and that teachers appear to preserve the
status quo. To be completely fair, though, teachers are tired. With
extra duties and responsibilities heaped upon them daily, they often
do not have the energy to rethink their teaching philosophy and
revamp their teaching methods. Yet I am amazed at the number of
teachers I've worked with who, in spite of their heavy teaching loads,
continue to be enthusiastic about new ideas and who want to try new
things in their classrooms. It's to them and others like them that I
direct this book, with the hope that they may find in it something to
make their own, and something to give their students.

An anecdote is in order here. As a brand-new teacher in the late 1970s, I was introduced to young adult literature by our high school librarian, who had attended an in-service workshop at which Robert Cormier spoke. She brought back copies of *The Chocolate War* and *I Am the Cheese*, along with a flyer containing biographical information about the author, and gave them to me to read. I was hooked. However, I taught at a small school in a conservative community, and, being a new teacher, I feared the challenges I might face if I assigned such books to my ninth graders. Then I discovered that my colleague down the hall— also a new teacher—was using S. E. Hinton's *The Outsiders* with his eighth graders and having great success with it. He had received no complaints from administrators or parents, in spite of the fact that he had violated a district rule against asking students to buy extra books for their classes. So I went out on a limb, and, with our librarian as my co-conspirator, smuggled in copies of Paul Zindel's *The Pigman*, which I read on my colleague's recommendation and which I in my insecurity felt was less controversial than Cormier's books. Teaching that book was my first *real* experience teaching literature. The students were extraordinarily responsive, and I was changed forever as a teacher. In fact, my excitement resulted in the creation of a new independent reading course that still survives in that school's curriculum.

I tell this story to encourage you to have faith in your convictions, to venture out on a limb once in a while, to make a difference in your students' academic lives. Listening to the voices of students as they read may help us hear our own voices as we teach. Are we responding to the literature from our hearts, or are we responding only from our heads, saying what we think we're expected to say? If we continue to be conscious of such things as we study literature with our students, the work of Dora Smith and others will not have been in vain. Though the wheels of educational change turn slowly, they do continue to turn, thanks to teachers who are willing to work to effect change. If Dora Smith were here today, I'm sure she'd be amazed at how far young adult literature has come as a literary genre and proud of the role she played in its development. She did her part; now it's up to us to do ours.

Works Cited

Stover, L. T. 1996. *Young Adult Literature: The Heart of the Middle School Curriculum*. Portsmouth, NH: Boynton/Cook.

Wood, G. H. 1992. *Schools That Work: America's Most Innovative Public Education Programs*. New York: Penguin.

DATE DUE